S0-BKS-406

► *A hiker surveys Colorado National Monument.* JEFF GNASS

Staying in touch with the Colorado Geographic Series

Falcon Press brings you the talent of America's best outdoor photographers and the knowledge of the best writers in the Colorado Geographic Series.

Each book explores a different facet of Colorado in magnificent, full-color photos and clear, concise text that will instruct as well as entertain you. Look for future publications examining the state's geology, history, culture, natural resources, recreation, and scenic grandeur. All books in the Colorado Geographic Series are similar in format and quality to this book.

For information on books and calendars published by Falcon Press, write for a free catalog to Falcon Press, P.O. Box 1718, Helena, MT 59103, or call 1-800-582-BOOK (outside Montana) 1-800-592-BOOK (in Montana).

COLORADO geographic series

► *Mountain wood lily blooms orange and red near Cub Lake Trail in Rocky Mountain National Park.* JAMES FRANK

C O L O R A D O
PARKLANDS

NUMBER FIVE COLORADO GEOGRAPHIC SERIES BY STEWART M. GREEN

► *Transformed by the luminous light of the setting sun, clouds over Longs Peak reflect intense color.* JOE ARNOLD JR.

Colorado Geographic Series staff

Publishers: Michael S. Sample,
 Bill Schneider
Editor: Marnie Hagmann
Photo editor: Jeri Walton
Design and layout: DD Dowden
Cartography: DD Dowden
Marketing director: Kelly Simmons

Front cover photo

David Hiser/Photographers Aspen

Back cover photos

Left, David Hiser/Photographers Aspen; top right, Larry Pierce; bottom right, Tom Bean

Copyright © 1988 by Falcon Press Publishing Co., Inc., Helena and Billings, Montana.

All rights reserved, including the right to reproduce this book in any form, except brief quotations for reviews, without the written permission of the publisher.

Library of Congress Number: 86-82747
ISBN 0-937959-37-5 (softcover)
ISBN 0-937959-38-3 (hardcover)

Design, typesetting, and other prepress work by Falcon Press, Helena, Montana.

Printed in Hong Kong.

Acknowledgments

The fabric of *Colorado Parklands* is woven from many disparate threads. It took a drawer full of bulging file folders and a lot of interviews to write this book. First, I thank the park rangers and managers at Colorado's many parks who graciously and patiently answered my questions, showed me around, and otherwise helped out. An extra thanks to Bob Schultz and Dan Brown at Curecanti National Recreation Area, Monica Miller with the Colorado Division of Parks and Outdoor Recreation, Glen Kaye at Rocky Mountain National Park, Howard Dimont at Mesa Verde National Park, Alan Whalon at Hovenweep National Monument, John Welch and Ann Schaffer at Dinosaur National Monument, Arthur Cuthair at Ute Mountain Tribal Park, Susan Trumble at Roxborough State Park, Bob Toll at Eldorado Canyon State Park, Carol Leasure at Barr Lake State Park, Craig Bergman at Lory State Park, Michael Hopper at State Forest State Park, Larry Haines at Navajo State Recreation Area, Ron Dunlap at Cherry Creek State Recreation Area, Rick Severson at the Garden of the Gods, Rich Koopman at Boulder County Parks, Brian Peck at Boulder Mountain Parks, and Chris Wilson at Boulder Open Space. I also wish to thank Colorado Springs geologist Sue Raabe who shared her research on the Royal Gorge and Temple Canyon and Ed Webster who gave extra info on climbing around Boulder.

Editors are the people behind the scenes—they make a good book better. For that I'm grateful to Falcon Press editor Marnie Hagmann in Helena, Montana, who made valuable comments, suggestions, and criticisms. It shows in the finished manuscript. Thanks also to Hewlett-Packard editor Janet Smith for help when needed.

Thanks to Bill Schneider, Falcon Press publisher, for the opportunity to contribute to the outstanding Colorado Geographic Series, to DD Dowden who designed the book, and to Falcon Press publisher Mike Sample and photo editor Jeri Walton who labored over thousands of transparencies.

Finally, thanks to my family—Nancy, Ian, and Brett—for companionship on field trips, for giving uninterrupted time, and for patience and support.

About the author

Writer and photographer Stewart M. Green is a Colorado Springs native. He is the author of *Pikes Peak Country: The Complete Guide,* and his photographs have been widely published in Sierra Club calendars and *Sierra, Outside, National Motorist,* and *National Wildlife* magazines. Readers will also recognize Green's excellent photography from previous books in the Colorado Geographic Series.

CONTENTS

JEFF FOOTT

INTRODUCTION
COLORADO PARKLANDS

A hush falls over Eleven Mile State Recreation Area just before sunrise. Mountains rise beyond the lake's inlet, their summits shimmering above grassy South Park. A fisherman stands on the shoreline and casts his line far out, its splash rippling the lake's stillness.

An immense silence fills Colorado National Monument's Ute Canyon. The melodic notes of a canyon wren ring off the sandstone walls. Two hikers take a last drink of water, shoulder their packs, and set off into the morning quiet.

The sun is just rising now. At Cherry Creek State Recreation Area a windsurfer stretches in its warmth and then pushes into the cool water to test the morning wind.

Farther north, Longs Peak glows ruddy in Chasm Lake. Cold mountain air streams down from the Continental Divide in Rocky Mountain National Park, invigorating a family at Moraine Park Campground. The smell of fresh coffee mingles with the butterscotch scent of the surrounding ponderosa pines.

And at Great Sand Dunes National Monument, a lone figure greets the dawn with outstretched arms from the crest of the highest dune. Sunlight creeps across the dune field, washing it with gold and etching dark shadows in its folds.

Each scene is from Colorado's parklands, and each is a reflection of the state's scenic and recreational diversity. Many associate the word "park" with a carefully manicured, grassy area. In the formal European tradition, parks were landscaped with flowers, trees, grass, and fountains. Today, the definition of a park is wider. Parks are landscapes that are not only ordered and tended by man, but wildlands as well, just as nature made them. Parks are also political entities. They are set aside by federal, state, and local governments to preserve and protect unique natural and cultural areas and to provide opportunities for outdoor recreation.

Colorado's parklands, totaling almost one million acres (that's one-third larger than Rhode Island), include two national parks, seven national monuments, eleven state parks, one national recreation area, twenty-three state recreation areas, eight major urban park systems, and a host of city parks. Protected within Colorado's parks are archaeological wonders, pristine ecosystems with rare plants and animals, unique geologic features, lakes that provide a wide range of recreation, and urban parks that offer open space, give scenic views, and bring park experiences to people living in Colorado's cities.

Our parks are managed by different agencies—the National Park Service, the Colorado Division of Parks and Outdoor Recreation, and various county and city park and recreation departments—that all have the same basic goal: to preserve parklands for future generations and to manage public use.

"We have to provide a balance between preservation and use," says Bob Schultz, Chief Naturalist at Curecanti National Recreation Area. "That's what makes it so tough. We have to use the resource, but not use it up. But the function of all park units, to a degree, is recreation. Parks are a break from one's day-to-day routine and a place for people to learn about the world."

Learning about the world—that's a primary mission of Colorado's parklands. Enos Mills, writer, naturalist, and father of Rocky Mountain National Park, would have agreed with Schultz. In 1917 Mills wrote: "Investments in outdoor vacations give large returns; from an outing one returns with life lengthened, in livelier spirits, more efficient, with new ideas and a broader outlook, and more hopeful and kind. Hence parks and outdoor recreation places are mighty factors for the general welfare; they assist in making better men and women."

Colorado Parklands helps you discover, explore, enjoy, and understand our diverse park system. Go. There's a whole world out there waiting. ∎

► *The rising sun peeks through morning clouds shrouding the Puma Hills above Eleven Mile State Recreation Area, top left, fifty miles west of Colorado Springs.* STEWART M. GREEN

► *Loveable mule deer, top right, flourish in Boulder's urban parklands, which spread across 32,000 acres of mountains and prairies.* STEWART M. GREEN.

► *Marsh marigolds, bottom left, a favorite food of elk, carpet subalpine streamsides with large, white-petaled flowers in Colorado's mountain parks.*
MICHAEL S. SAMPLE

*You are not wood, you are
not stones, but men.*
—SHAKESPEARE

ANASAZI PARKLANDS

THE INDIAN PARKS

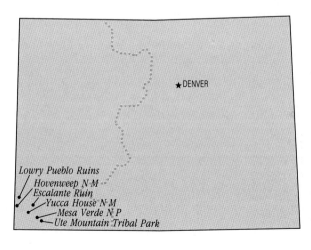

Lowry Pueblo Ruins
Hovenweep N·M
Escalante Ruin
Yucca House N·M
Mesa Verde N·P
Ute Mountain Tribal Park

★DENVER

For seven centuries the ruins have lain hidden in their canyon aeries, their windows and doors dark with shadow, their plazas empty, their walls crumbled by wind and rain. Once these houses were filled with the sounds of laughter, song, and prayer.

Who were these people? Navajos, entering southwestern Colorado in the late fourteenth century, called them *Anasazi,* "the ancient ones." Although they left Colorado in the late 1200s, the Anasazi were neither a lost civilization nor race. Indeed, the people endured, settling on the fertile banks of the Rio Grande in New Mexico and on mesas in Arizona. Their modern-day descendants, the Hopi Indians, call them *Hisatsinom,* "the long ago people."

The Anasazi were short with straight black hair. The men averaged five feet four inches in height, while the women reached five feet. They had a strong aesthetic sense, an eye for style and grace, seen in their neatly coiled baskets, decorated pottery, jewelry with turquoise beads, and shells traded from the Gulf of Mexico and the Pacific Coast. They made music with flutes carved from the wing bones of eagles.

They never invented the wheel, used draft animals, or developed a written language, but they did incorporate solar principles into their architecture and devised methods to chart the movements of the sun and moon. Religion was important in their daily lives. Look at Cliff Palace with its twenty-three kivas, or underground ceremonial chambers, and imagine an American town of 250 people today with twenty-three churches.

They were also accustomed to death. Almost 50 percent of all babies died before they reached the age of five. Old age quickly crept up on the Anasazi. By age thirty-four most were dead, and those who lived on were wracked by rheumatism and arthritis and pained by teeth worn to the gums by a lifetime of chewing grit mixed in their cornmeal.

Perhaps 15,000 years ago the Anasazi crossed the Bering land bridge from Asia to America. By the time of Christ, they had settled in Colorado, hunting game, following herds of deer and bighorn sheep, and gathering roots, tubers, berries, cacti, and nuts.

Over the next few centuries, they began sowing corn and squash and weaving baskets and bags. Growing dependent on agriculture, the Anasazi settled in villages, building cozy pithouses, semisubterranean rooms roofed with branches and mud mortar, alongside their fields.

As their neighbors in New Mexico acquired new tools and skills, the Anasazi were quick to adopt them. By A.D. 750 the bow and arrow had replaced the *atlatl,* a primitive dart-throwing hunting stick. They domesticated turkeys for food and wove warm blankets from the feathers.

Around the same time the Anasazi moved out of the earth and built villages on mesa-tops with stones and mortar. During the next 600 years they built sophisticated buildings with quarried stone plastered smooth with mud mortar, some reaching three and even four stories high.

Between 700 and 1300 women created pottery with distinctive styles and decorations in a variety of shapes and sizes, including mugs, ollas (large storage vessels), bowls, and jars.

Despite outward appearances, however, all was not well with the Anasazi. During the late 1200s they simply left. The great exodus was over by 1300, and the once bustling cities fell into disrepair and ruin. The Anasazi moved south, settling in New Mexico and Arizona where their historic descendants, the Pueblo and Hopi Indians, live today.

The Anasazi left not only their stone cities behind but also an intriguing mystery: Why did they go? Perhaps the prolonged drought from 1276 to 1299 forced them to find better-watered lands. Perhaps it was soil depletion from generations farming the same plots. Perhaps the Anasazi overhunted the game animals in the area. Archaeologists say it was probably a combination of all these factors.

Whatever the reasons, they must have been compelling. For the Anasazi deserted Colorado forever, leaving behind clay bowls, baskets filled with seed corn, gardening tools, and their homeland of a thousand years. Now the remains of their civilization are preserved in Colorado's Anasazi parklands—Mesa Verde National Park, Hovenweep National Monument, Ute Mountain Tribal Park, Yucca House National Monument, and Lowry Pueblo Ruins—places full of mystery and wonder.

► *Evening clouds flame with day's last light over Cajon Mesa in Hovenweep National Monument along the Colorado-Utah border.* STEWART M. GREEN

► *Petroglyphs adorn a sandstone wall along Petroglyph Point Trail in Mesa Verde National Park.* RANDY TRINE

MESA VERDE NATIONAL PARK

December 18, 1888, dawned cold and cloudy. Swirling snow filled the air, covering the canyons and plateaus of Mesa Verde with a soft, white blanket. Two cowboys, Richard Wetherill and Charles Mason, were searching the dense woodland atop the mesa for stray cattle.

As residents in the area since 1879, the men had come upon numerous ruined cliff villages. In 1874 an eight-man Hayden Geological and Geographical Survey party, including the famed photographer William Henry Jackson, had discovered the first Mesa Verde dwelling to be named and photographed—Two-Story Cliff House. Jackson later wrote, "In the extreme southwestern corner of Colorado Territory...are groups of old ruined homes and towns, displaying a civilization and intelligence far beyond that of any present inhabitants of this or adjacent territory."

But it wasn't until that winter day in 1888 that the two cowboys stumbled upon the grandest cliff dwelling of all and Mesa Verde was transformed from a remote plateau to America's most famous archaeological wonder. Acowitz, a Ute friend, had told Wetherill that one house, far bigger than the others, stood high in the rocks. It was a sacred place, however, and to go there would profane the dead and bring their misfortune upon yourself.

Imagine the astonishment of Wetherill and Mason to see that silent, empty city of stone tucked under a cave across Cliff Canyon. Using their lariats to lash several trees together, the men descended the makeshift ladder to the canyon bottom. After climbing up to the ruin, they stood in wonder and awe. All around them rose crumbled walls, half hidden by fallen rubble. In the middle stood a round tower.

Walking about, the men disturbed dust that had collected for 700 years. The city looked as if its residents had only temporarily left. Whole pots and stone tools sat on walls. Years later Charles Mason told the story in the *Denver Post*, "We spent several hours going from room to room, and picked up several articles of interest, among them a stone axe with the handle still on it. There were also parts of several human skeletons scattered about." That same day Wetherill dubbed their discovery Cliff Palace.

Today, Cliff Palace remains the glittering crown jewel in what is now Mesa Verde National Park. It's the largest cliff dwelling in the park, which contains more than 4,000 prehistoric sites, including almost 600 nested, like Cliff Palace, in the sandstone cliffs. Only 200 of the park's sites are named, and less than 50 have been excavated.

Mesa Verde, America's only national park set aside to preserve archaeological sites, was created in 1906 to protect its ancient cities from theft and destruction by pothunters and tourists. That same year a Federal Antiquities Act became law, protecting archaeological sites on federal lands. In 1978 Mesa Verde was recognized by the United Nations Educational, Scientific, and Cultural Organization (UNESCO) as an important

► *A vaulted stone arch encloses Cliff Palace, the largest Anasazi cliff village in Mesa Verde. This 200-room site discovered by cowboys Richard Wetherill and Charles Mason in 1888 was only occupied about seventy-five years until the mesa was abandoned in 1300.* ED COOPER

part of our global heritage and named the U.S.'s first World Heritage Cultural Site.

The park encompasses 52,000 acres of a high plateau the Spanish called Mesa Verde—the green tableland. Rising abruptly above the Montezuma and Mancos valleys, seven miles southeast of Cortez, its steep sides, capped by sandstone cliffs, form a natural fortress. The plateau is almost impenetrable except along the Mancos River, which sheers through the barrier from east to west.

From Park Point, Mesa Verde's highest peak at 8,571 feet, the plateau gently dips to the south to 6,969 feet at park headquarters. This gentle tilt to the south makes the mesa as much as twenty degrees warmer than in Cortez, a thousand feet lower. A 155-day growing season, eighteen inches of annual rainfall divided between winter snows and summer thunderstorms, and fertile soil give ideal growing conditions for beans, corn, and squash.

Besides being an archaeological wonder, Mesa Verde also harbors many animals in its rugged vastness. Almost 16 percent of the park is designated wilderness, and public access to the rest is severely restricted, leaving many undisturbed areas for wildlife. Mountain lions, small herds of bighorn sheep and elk, occasional black bears, and a large herd of mule deer live in the park. Over 175 bird species, including eagles and prairie and peregrine falcons, have been identified. Cliff Palace milk vetch, a rare plant in the pea family, lives only on Chapin and Moccasin mesas.

► *Mountain lions, above left, range across Mesa Verde's 52,000 acres, subsisting mainly on the park's abundant mule deer population.* W. PERRY CONWAY

► *Cliff Canyon abruptly slices into Mesa Verde's high plateau, above right. Alcoves and caves in the steep Cliff House sandstone below the canyon rims once housed the Anasazi.* STEWART M. GREEN

But it's the Anasazi cliff dwellings that people come to marvel at. Visitors follow a paved road twenty-one miles from the park entrance seven miles east of Cortez off U.S. 160 to Chapin Mesa, site of the most famous ruins and the park museum.

After entering the park, visitors first encounter a spectacular panoramic view unfolding from Park Point. Distant mountains rim the horizon: the Abajo Mountains in Utah; the San Miguel Range; and pointy Mount Hesperus in the La Plata Mountains. To the south, Shiprock rises like an apparition from the Navajo Reservation, and beyond it lie the hazy Chuska Mountains in Arizona. To the west towers Sleeping Ute Mountain, spreading its long bulk above the Montezuma Valley.

Beyond Park Point the road passes the first Anasazi site—Far View Ruins.

Exhibiting the park's best mesa-top architecture, this ancient city sheltered a large population in fifty dwelling sites spread over a half a square mile from A.D. 900 to 1300. Far View House, a rectangular pueblo with about fifty rooms and five kivas, possibly reached four stories high and probably resembled Taos Pueblo, a modern counterpart in New Mexico. This area was densely occupied because it receives more rainfall than the southern part of Mesa Verde.

Water was the blood of the Anasazi lifeway. Water grew vital crops—beans, squash, and corn—and freed the Anasazi from the constant task of finding food. They planted crops on the mesa tops and built check dams to slow the runoff from summer storms. Mainly, however, they depended on dry-land farming.

Mummy Lake at Far View Ruins was

possibly a water-storage system. This small reservoir, ninety feet in diameter and twelve feet deep, was capable of storing half a million gallons of water. Whether it ever contained water, though, is a matter of speculation. Some archaeologists believe an irrigation channel, the Far View Ditch, allowed water to flow five miles down the mesa to the head of Spruce Canyon. Others think there was no irrigation channel there at all.

From Far View Ruins the road drops onto Chapin Mesa, a long finger of land between Spruce and Soda canyons, where Spruce Tree House, Square Tower House, Cliff Palace, Balcony House, and the park museum are located. A series of dioramas built by the Civilian Conservation Corps in the 1930s depicting the different stages of Indian habitation of the region from paleo-

► *Silence fills the ancient rooms in Square Tower House clustered beneath an overhanging cliff in Mesa Verde's Navajo Canyon. The village, home to 100 or so Indians, bustled with activity during its thirteenth-century heyday.* LARRY BURTON

hunters tracking bison to life in Spruce Tree House during the Anasazi golden age makes a good introduction to the park. Other displays of basketry, pottery, tools, clothing, and architecture help bring the deserted cities to life.

Spruce Tree House, the third-largest cliff dwelling, is the park's best preserved ruin. Located in an alcove of Spruce Canyon below the museum, it is protected from both summer rain and winter snow. The village housed about 125 people in 114 rooms and eight kivas. A nearby year-round spring was undoubtedly important to Spruce Tree House's residents.

Square Tower House is one of the most spectacular cliff dwellings. Nestled in a shallow cave, it imparts a quiet human dignity to wild Navajo Canyon. One wall on the square tower, the park's tallest structure, measures thirty-three feet high. The pueblo has about eighty remaining rooms and seven kivas. Two of the kivas have partially intact roofs, a rarity because of the natural aging process and the overzealous efforts of pothunters.

Cliff Palace, looking more like a Hollywood set than one of America's greatest archaeological wonders, lies sheltered in an arching alcove. Up to 250 Indians called Cliff Palace home during its brief efflorescence. Based on tree-ring data from the ruin, archaeologists say it

was built between 1209 and 1273 and may have been occupied until 1300. The site today has 217 rooms and twenty-three kivas that sprawl across the yawning 325-foot-wide cave mouth. Cliff Palace is one of Mesa Verde's few sites that can be visited without a guide during the

summer season.

While Cliff Palace stuns visitors with its size and sophistication, Balcony House thrills them with its sheer dropoffs. Before embarking on the ranger-led tour of the thirty-five-to-forty-room ruin, visitors are warned of tall ladders,

▶ *Majestic bald eagles nest in remote canyons deep in Mesa Verde's rugged backcountry.*
JEFF FOOTT

chopped stairs, and vertical cliffs. The tour involves climbing a thirty-two-foot ladder into the ruin and then exiting via a crawl passageway and several ladders to the canyon rim.

The most defensible of the park's larger ruins, Balcony House had only one entryway along a 400-foot-long ledge, spring water in the cave, and a cliff facade. Its inhabitants came and went on toeholds carved into the rock face itself. But despite its obvious defense characteristics, no evidence indicates the Anasazi here were ever threatened.

Wetherill Mesa, three miles west of Chapin Mesa, has a group of ruins that can be visited by way of a narrow, winding twelve-mile-long road, closed in winter, that begins at the Far View Visitor Center area. In 1987 only 43,000 visitors made the trip to Wetherill, compared with the 720,000 that visited Chapin Mesa.

Wetherill was opened to the public in the mid-1970s after the completion of the Wetherill Mesa Archaeological Project, a ten-year exploration of Mesa Verde's prehistory. In addition to archaeologists, scientists from twenty-seven other specialties, including geology, biology, ecology, and medicine, conducted the most thorough examination of the Anasazi ever undertaken. The results gave an almost complete picture of life on Mesa Verde from A.D. 600 to 1300.

Visitors to Wetherill walk through two excavated cliff dwellings—Long House and Step House—and see several mesa-top sites, including pithouse and pueblo ruins. Long House, the second largest "city" in the park, once had about 150 rooms and twenty-one kivas with an

approximate population of 200. An exact room count is impossible because the site was extensively damaged by pothunting and vandalism in the nineteenth century. Dynamite fuses were even found among the rubble before excavation.

For seven full centuries Mesa Verde saw the flowering of a unique and creative people. These people struggled to nurture their corn on this dry, unyielding land. They mastered water, controlling its meager flow to nourish their fields. They lifted themselves up from the earth, building huge "apartment buildings" that were unequaled in size in the United States until the 1870s.

Between 3,000 and 5,000 Indians might have lived on this now desolate mesa, with as many as 25,000 to 30,000 in the neighboring Montezuma Valley.

Clearly, these were people building for the future, filling the canyons with the noise, excitement, and motion of a burgeoning civilization. And then they moved away, leaving their bowls, mugs, and tools, and abandoning their homeland of generations. For seven centuries the crumbling cities endured, guarded only by cliffs and canyons. Until one snowy December day in 1888, two cowboys discovered the grandest cliff palace of all and brought the Anasazi back to the future.

► *Masonry walls in Long House, left, Mesa Verde's second-largest ruin, meld with the soaring sandstone amphitheater overhead. Long House, with twenty-one kivas and a dance plaza, may have been a place where Anasazi clans crowded together on ceremonial occasions.* STEWART M. GREEN

► *Visitors study a reconstructed pithouse on Wetherill Mesa, right. Semisubterranean pithouses offered warm shelter through Mesa Verde's chilly winters from 550 A.D to 750 A.D. Entry was usually through the smoke-hole in the roof.* STEWART M. GREEN

HOVENWEEP NATIONAL MONUMENT

► *A glare of sun silhouettes Hovenweep Castle at Hovenweep National Monument.* STEWART M. GREEN

Cajon Mesa, a 500-square-mile tableland, spreads west from Cortez in southwestern Colorado onto the arid badlands above the San Juan River in southeastern Utah. The sage and juniper-covered mesa breaks with shallow canyons rimmed by sandstone cliffs and laced with scant creeks—Yellowjacket, Cross, Hovenweep, Bridge, and Ruin—that thread south to the San Juan River. Along the canyon heads stand deserted, thousand-year-old villages built by "the ancient ones," the Anasazi Indians.

The ruins are close to water, the lifeblood of the desert. Towers guard precious springs that percolate from bedrock. Multiroom community houses stand on the canyon rims next to farming plots. Protecting the largest and best preserved of these towers and pueblos scattered along the Colorado-Utah border is 785-acre Hovenweep National Monument with its six ruin groups: Square Tower, Cajon, Holly, Hackberry-Horseshoe, Cutthroat Castle, and Goodman Point ruins. The 1923 proclamation that established the monument said the ruins had "the finest prehistoric masonry in the United States."

Today Hovenweep might be Colorado's loneliest parkland. The name itself means "deserted valley," a Ute word given by photographer William Henry Jackson, when his Hayden Survey party explored the region in 1874. Traveling west down McElmo Canyon from today's Cortez, Jackson noted "small cave-

► *Four mule deer bucks lock antlers in an autumn battle. Common to most Colorado parks, mule deer were an important food source for the ancient Anasazi.* W. PERRY CONWAY

houses'' in the cliffs and observed towers on the canyon rims.

A sleepiness blankets Hovenweep National Monument. A few dusty ranches, dryland farms, and oil wells dot the arid landscape, bleached by sunlight and scoured by wind. Thirty miles northeast

of Hovenweep's ranger station, the town of Dove Creek bills itself as ''pinto bean capital of the world.'' Cortez lies almost forty miles east of Hovenweep. Yet, this barren land bustled with activity more than a thousand years ago.

Not a lot of research has delved into the

Anasazi who inhabited Hovenweep's mesas and canyons. Archaeologists have been more interested in Mesa Verde's grand cliff dwellings and the pueblos around Cortez than in these backroad ruins. In 1917-18 archaeologist Jesse Fewkes of the Smithsonian Institution

► *Twin Towers, far left, a sixteen-room pueblo, overlooks Hovenweep's Little Ruin Canyon. Hovenweep's towers are its great mystery. Perhaps they guarded precious springs, protected their pastoral people, or charted the course of the sun and stars. No one knows. By 1300 the Anasazi had abandoned this homeland of 700 years.* STEWART M. GREEN

► *Perched on a canyon rim, Cutthroat Castle's high walls blend with bedrock, left. The ruin, accessible by trail, is Hovenweep's most remote site.* STEWART M. GREEN

surveyed the Hovenweep area and recommended its protection as a national monument. No comprehensive archaeological work has been conducted since.

We do know that Hovenweep's Anasazi had the same culture as their Mesa Verde neighbors fifty miles to the east. Settled by the Basketmaker Anasazi, Hovenweep had numerous small villages by A.D. 750. These villages, probably occupied by extended family groups, dotted the mesa-tops near their farming plots. Later, from 1150 to 1300, the Indians clustered together, building community houses along the canyon rims near permanent springs. Cajon Mesa and its drainages have nineteen major pueblos, with many more villages scattered between them. The best

preserved pueblos are found in the national monument.

By manipulating the area's scant water resources, the Anasazi successfully grew corn, beans, and squash in sandy fields and hillside terraces. To conserve water in this land of marginal rainfall, they built small reservoirs and check dams. The ruins on sloping Cajon Mesa receive varying amounts of precipitation, depending on elevation. At the highest ruin, 5,880-foot Cutthroat Castle, rainfall averages thirteen inches annually. Square Tower Ruins at 5,220 feet receives eleven inches, and Cajon Ruin, Hovenweep's lowest site at 5,150 feet, receives a scant nine inches of annual rainfall.

Hovenweep's towers and castles, built between 1163 and 1277, have alternately

▶ Sunflowers typically spread a showy display across Colorado's lower elevations in July and August. MICHAEL S. SAMPLE

confused and fascinated both archaeologists and visitors. Today hundreds of the round, square, and D-shaped towers survive along the canyon rims. Perhaps the best example is Square Tower at Square Tower Ruins. Its graceful walls of quarried stone rise three stories above a solitary entrance.

Why the Anasazi erected these towers is Hovenweep's great mystery. At first sight, they appear as impregnable fortresses poised above the canyons, perhaps guarding a failing water supply or warding off enemies. Archaeologists suggest the towers were for defense because of their strategic locations near springs and canyon heads and their few doors and windows. "There is definitely a defensive feeling to the towers," says Alan Whalon, Hovenweep's Area Manager, "but not much evidence supports hostile Indians moving through here."

Other possible tower uses include food storage, line-of-sight communication, ceremonial uses, or astronomical observations. It was important for an agricultural people like the Anasazi to follow the seasons for planting and harvesting their crops. Archaeologists, plotting the movement of sunbeams through windows on interior walls in some towers, suggest the towers marked the winter and summer solstices and the spring and autumn equinoxes. Out of dozens of sites, however, only Hovenweep Castle, Unit-type House, and Cajon Ruin have portals that could be used for calendric purposes.

The largest, best preserved, and most visited of the six monument units is the Square Tower Group. A 1974 field survey located sixty-eight archaeological sites, spanning 9,000 years of prehistory, scattered over 400 acres. Five large ruin complexes, including Hovenweep Castle, Square Tower, and Stronghold House, have been excavated and stabilized. The Square Tower unit, Hovenweep's largest, sees over 80 percent of the monument's 16,000 annual visitors.

The monument's other ruins are little known and rarely visited. Horseshoe Ruin, five miles east of Square Tower, contains some of Hovenweep's best masonry. Under the ruin, muddy handprints spot a cave's wall, relics of the Anasazi's passage through time.

Holly Ruins, a mile from Horseshoe, includes the tallest free-standing Anasazi wall, at twenty-five feet, in Colorado. Inside the Holly Great House archaeologists found a plastered floor with a firepit, grinding stones, and a storage jar containing 175 animal bones, including collared lizard, western spadefoot toad, cottontail rabbit, and other bird, reptile, and rodent bones.

On the southern edge of Cajon Mesa, ten miles southwest of Square Tower, Cajon Ruin sprawls across the head of a steep arroyo. This is a pueblo with a view—striped badlands ridge the San Juan River below, and distant buttes in Arizona's Monument Valley punctuate the flat horizon. To harness the area's meager water, the Anasazi built a rock and earthen dam in the gully above the village.

Cutthroat Castle, eleven miles northeast of Square Tower, is a compact pueblo perched above a shallow canyon. A kiva hangs on a cliff edge, and a round tower overlooks the canyon. Cutthroat is a quiet, crumbling ruin, its shattered walls the home of lizards, owls, and Anasazi ghosts.

Hovenweep gives a view of the Anasazi different from Mesa Verde. It's a place to let your imagination run free: walk into an unexcavated ruin, sit on a stone wall, and feel the presence of the ancient ones. Children shout across the village plaza, gossiping women grind corn on the rimrock, hunters return from a successful hunt. "We offer a sense of discovery at Hovenweep," says Whalon. "You have more freedom to wander around here, unlike Mesa Verde where you're controlled. Visitors have more intimate contact with the Anasazi culture at Hovenweep. It's important that we protect the cultural setting here, so we try to keep signs away from the ruins and try to maintain a sense of them being untouched. We're trying to keep the monument undeveloped."

But the winds of change blow here as surely as desert wind sweeps out of dry canyons. Already Colorado and Utah plan to pave the twenty-five-mile dirt road from Pleasant View to Hovenweep. With road improvements, the park expects visitation to soar. The National Park Service is also looking to expand Hovenweep, particularly the Square Tower unit. Says Whalon, "Since 1923 when Hovenweep became a national monument, archaeology has grown as a science. While we know the main ruin groups are important, the earlier sites on the mesas are equally important. We need to protect them to establish the cultural continuum from the earliest to the most recent sites, only then can we begin to know what happened here."

Oblivious to the controversy, the ruins at Hovenweep exude a quiet, dignified silence, a silence of the ages. When you venture out across the dusty roads, past the pumpkin-colored hills, you enter into a land of immense views and unbroken horizons. Out there, the land is doused with a dry light that defines the desolation and beauty that is and was Hovenweep National Monument.

UTE MOUNTAIN TRIBAL PARK

Southwestern Colorado was Ute Indian territory when the first white settlers started filtering in around 1860. It still is today. The Utes, the last Indian tribe living in Colorado, own Ute Mountain Ute Indian Reservation, encompassing 558,000 acres in a wide strip south from Mesa Verde National Park to the New Mexico border and west from Durango to the Utah border.

The Mountain Utes have set aside 125,000 acres of this land as parkland to preserve canyons, mesas, and the unspoiled remains of the ancient Anasazi.

Ute Mountain Tribal Park opened in the late 1970s with the blessing of the late Chief Jack House. The chief, seeing the tribe's gas and oil reserves being depleted, realized the Mountain Utes needed to broaden their economic base. Before his death in 1971, he suggested opening the sacred land as a tribal park.

"Jack House, our last traditional chief, lived in Mancos Canyon in the nineteen twenties and thirties," says Park Superintendent Arthur Cuthair. "The park was his idea, and without his approval it never would have come into being.

"There was a lot of resentment from our older people. Though the Ancient Ones were not of our people, we have much respect for their past, and people felt it was wrong to disturb or exploit it." Most Utes now accept the park, says Cuthair, "because they see the respect we show for the ruins."

Even though Ute Mountain Tribal Park and Mesa Verde National Park claim a common prehistory, the Utes were determined to present a different experience of the Anasazi from their famous neighbor. While Mesa Verde's popular sites look like they're manicured for the pages of an A.D. 1250 issue of *Better Homes and Gardens,* the Ute park's ruins present an unfinished appearance. The rubble and litter of seven centuries submerge many of the walls.

"We don't want a commercialized park," says Cuthair. "We don't want this to be another Mesa Verde. We want to show our visitors not only where the Ancient Ones lived, we also want to give them a feeling of what it was like living here."

Indeed, when you walk through the

ruins, it's as though you're the first person to set foot in the rooms since their owners left them. Corncobs, potsherds, stone and bone tools, and bones, some human, litter the ground. Visitors, who must be accompanied by a hired Ute guide, are encouraged to touch the walls where the mason left his fingerprints in mud and to pick up pieces of an olla that carried water from a distant spring.

Four ruins—Lion House, Eagle Nest House, Morse V, and Tree House—are on the tour. Lion House, the largest in the park, nestles under an arching cave. It has forty-six rooms and six kivas. Eagle Nest House, reached by ladders, is a spectacular aerie tucked under the rimrock.

Beginning at Ute Mountain Indian Pottery at Towaoc on U.S. 160, the tour lasts seven or eight hours. Visitors drive their own cars on a fifty-five-mile-long dirt road to the cliff dwellings, stopping along the way at rock art sites and surface pueblos. Tours are by reservation only and are subject to cancellation by bad weather.

Mesa Verde visitors can also visit the tribal park where Ruins Road dips into it or by sightseeing helicopter. The park's season generally lasts from May through October. Only 1,800 people visited the park in 1986—three-tenths of 1 percent the number that visited Mesa Verde.

An awesome silence pervades the canyons at Ute Mountain. Close your eyes and listen to the quiet. You can hear the humanity of the crumpled walls. You can hear distant voices from another time speak to you heart to heart, soul to soul. Suddenly you're face to face with the world of yesterday.

OTHER INDIAN PARKS

Archaeologists say southwestern Colorado supported more people a thousand years ago than today. The land is literally covered with ruins. Mesa Verde's thousands of Anasazi sites represent only a small percentage of the number of ruins blanketing the Montezuma Valley west of the mesa. Farmers plow fields full of Anasazi villages. Eight huge "cities," populations ranging from 1,000 to 2,500 Indians, are scattered across the wide valley. The most impressive and largest sites are preserved as small parklands.

Lowry Pueblo Ruins, twenty miles northwest of Cortez, were built about A.D. 1090 by an Anasazi group closely related to those living in Chaco Canyon in west-central New Mexico. The forty-room pueblo was occupied for a scant fifty years and abandoned about 1140. The site's most unusual feature is a kiva painted with geometric designs.

Managed by the Bureau of Land Management (BLM) and registered as a National Historic Landmark, Lowry was named for early homesteader George Lowry. It was excavated in the 1930s by Paul S. Martin from the Chicago Field Museum of Natural History.

► *Mute testimony to their maker's skill and labor, Lowry Pueblo Ruins' timeworn walls reveal few secrets to park visitors. The pueblo's neatly quarried and laid stones contrast sharply with the rough masonry seen at nearby Mesa Verde.*
RANDY TRINE

► *Perched on a bluff, Escalante Ruin offers sweeping views of Montezuma Valley and Sleeping Ute Mountain. The ruin, discovered by Padres Escalante and Dominguez in 1776, was possibly built by Anasazi from Chaco Canyon, over 100 miles to the south.* STEWART M. GREEN

Escalante Ruin sits on the flat top of a broad hill overlooking McPhee Reservoir and the Montezuma Valley. Nine miles north of Cortez, it was the first of Colorado's Anasazi ruins to be described and reported. Its discoverers were Padres Escalante and Dominguez who came upon it while on their search for a trail from Santa Fe to the California missions. On the sixteenth day of their 1776 journey Escalante wrote: "Upon an elevation of the river's south side, there was in ancient times a small settlement of the same type as those of the Indians of New Mexico." The site was later named for Escalante, while a smaller nearby ruin was named for Dominguez. The twenty-five-room pueblo, built and inhabited in the late 1000s and abandoned by 1300, is laid out in the same style as the pueblos at Chaco Canyon in west-central New Mexico.

Dominguez Ruin, at the base of the hill below Escalante, held only four rooms and a single kiva. It was probably occupied by an extended family beginning in 1123. This small site yielded one of the Southwest's most notable burials. A man was found interred with a large collection of jewelry, personal belongings, and other grave goods.

Escalante and Dominguez ruins were excavated in the 1970s as part of the Dolores Archaeological Project, a federally funded program to study and preserve prehistoric sites affected by the construction of the McPhee Reservoir on the Dolores River. As part of the project, the Bureau of Reclamation built the Anasazi Heritage Center at the base of the hill below Escalante Ruin. Run by the BLM, it houses artifacts from Escalante as well as from sites excavated on surrounding land. Exhibits include a hands-on Discovery Area, a pithouse reconstruction, and other displays telling the story of southwest Colorado's first inhabitants. A paved half-mile trail leads to the ruins.

Yucca House National Monument is Colorado's most obscure federal parkland. The ten-acre site, ten miles southwest of Cortez, sits well off U.S. Highway 160 in the Montezuma Valley between Mesa Verde and Sleeping Ute Mountain. No highway signs mark the way to the ruin. The site, the remains of a large Anasazi pueblo, is being held "in reserve" for future archaeologists to excavate and study. The National Park Service discourages visiting the site, although directions and a one-page handout are available at Mesa Verde National Park.

Other Indian sites are scattered across Colorado. Arrowheads turn up in parks once frequented by the Plains Indians, such as Garden of the Gods and Red Rocks Park. The Arapahoes often used Rabbit Mountain Park, north of Boulder, as a winter campsite. Almost ninety tepee rings have been identified in the park. Trinidad State Recreation Area also has tepee rings on the bluffs above the lake left by nomadic Apaches. Evidence atop the Painted Wall, Colorado's tallest cliff, in the Black Canyon of the Gunnison National Monument indicates Utes camped on the canyon rim.

Dinosaur National Monument, with 404 recorded archaeological sites, was home to many Indians. Early man camped at the Deluge Shelter on Jones Creek, one of the monument's oldest sites, as long ago as 5,000 B.C. The Fremont Indians, a group similar to the Anasazi, occupied Dinosaur until A.D. 1150. They lived in semisubterranean pithouse villages, grew crops along the rivers and creeks, and left a stunning legacy of rock art on the canyon walls. The most unusual find in Dinosaur was a beautiful ermine headdress adorned with 350 black and orange feathers found buried in a leather pouch in Mantle Cave along the Yampa River.

Indians regularly occupied Roxborough State Park, south of Denver, over the last 5,000 years. Archaeologists date the earliest site at 5,500 B.C., with Indians continuing to inhabit the area until historic times. Designated a National Archaeological District, the park has over forty Indian sites hidden in its 1,500 acres. Among them are twelve campsites, three sheltered by the towering sandstone formations and the others in open valleys.

The Curecanti National Archaeological District lies in Curecanti National Recreation Area west of Gunnison. The district encompasses seventy-nine prehistoric sites on 6,750 acres above Blue Mesa Lake. The most significant find is the remains of a 4,500-year-old dwelling, one of the oldest in North America. The dwelling, possibly a tent or brush-covered structure, was probably used by a family group. Archaeologists uncovered fire pits, grinding stones, adobe, charcoal stains, and post-hole impressions at the site.

Colorado's Indian parks, preserving the campsites of long-ago hunters, the cliff palaces of sophisticated Anasazi masons, the mysterious rock art of the vanished Fremont Indians, and the tepee rings of nomadic wanderers, give our state a vital prehistory that rivals that of ancient Europe. Our Indian parklands are not

only an invaluable educational and scientific resource but places of wonder and awe as well. They were once filled with people who, like us, loved, laughed, cried, worked, cooked, and worried. If we listen closely to the stones and wood, we can feel their spirit. ▪

▶ *Anasazi handprints, smudging a cave wall under Hovenweep National Monument's Hackberry Ruin, preserve the memory of a long departed civilization. They ask us to remember that those who came before were not bricks and mortar, but men and women.* STEWART M. GREEN

<blockquote>
The finest workers in stone are... the gentle touches of air and water working at their leisure with a liberal allowance of time.
—HENRY DAVID THOREAU
</blockquote>

A STORY IN ROCKS

GEOLOGIC PARKS

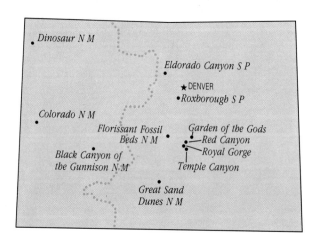

- Dinosaur N M
- Eldorado Canyon S P
- ★ DENVER
- Roxborough S P
- Colorado N M
- Florissant Fossil Beds N M
- Garden of the Gods
- Red Canyon
- Royal Gorge
- Black Canyon of the Gunnison N M
- Temple Canyon
- Great Sand Dunes N M

Colorado's landscape lies open like a great geologic book documenting the earth's long history. Rock layers and formations tell tales of different ages and landscapes, of towering mountains and quiet seas, of rocky canyons and wide rivers, of timelessness and eternal change. Some chapters are missing, washed away by erosion; others are so complex only trained earth scientists can decipher them. Colorado's geologic parklands preserve, protect, and help interpret this rock record.

The land we call Colorado is ancient. Rocks near Dinosaur National Monument in the far northwestern corner of the state are an amazing 2.3 billion years old—almost half the estimated age of the earth. Other rocks, those forming the valley floors at Colorado National Monument and the sheer cliffs of Black Canyon of the Gunnison National Monument, are 1.5 billion years old. These rocks were once sedimentary layers deposited on an ancient seafloor. Later heat and pressure squeezed, bent, and deformed the layers to form the metamorphic rocks we see today.

Over a billion years of erosion leveled Colorado's earliest mountains to their roots, leaving a flat, featureless plain. Beginning some 330 million years ago, new mountains rose out of the shallow sea that covered Colorado. These Ancestral Rockies, precursors to today's mountains, were two ranges—Frontrangia and Uncompahgria. Streams and rivers wore them down and spread a 1,500-foot-thick wedge-shaped layer of coarse sand and gravel in alluvial fans at their feet. The alluvium hardened underground over the next 150 million years into sandstone before being uplifted in the next mountain-building episode, called the Laramide Orogeny by geologists, about 65 million years ago. This laid the backbone of today's Rocky Mountains. The sandstone layers deposited at the foot of Frontrangia are visible in Eldorado Canyon and Roxborough state parks, Garden of the Gods Park, and Red Canyon Park.

Dinosaur and Colorado national monuments exhibit sandstone, siltstone, and mudstone layers deposited alongside Uncompahgria. One of the most famous is the Morrison Formation in Dinosaur National Monument. Thousands of dinosaur bones have been exhumed from the tilted Morrison sandstone, taking visitors back 140 million years to the age of reptiles.

A long period of stability followed the Laramide Orogeny until 30 million years ago when regional uplifts began raising Colorado to its present elevation. During this period magma pushed its way to the surface, spreading lava flows across the land and spewing vast quantities of ash and dust into the air. Thirtynine Mile Volcano, fifty miles west of Colorado Springs, violently erupted many times over 500,000 years and dramatically altered surrounding ecosystems, including that of prehistoric Lake Florissant at today's Florissant Fossil Beds National Monument. Here, preserved in thin ash layers, are the fossilized remains of insects, spiders, fish, and plants.

As today's Rockies rose, at least four periods of glaciation chipped away at them. Rivers, swollen with runoff from melting ice, sliced into bedrock to create Colorado's distinctive canyons. The most dramatic of these are preserved in Black Canyon, Colorado, and Dinosaur national monuments, Eldorado Canyon State Park, Royal Gorge Park, and Temple Canyon Park. The dunes at Great Sand Dunes National Monument, Colorado's most recent geologic feature, are also related to glaciation. The ancestral Rio Grande, filled with meltwater, left levees of sand on its banks that the wind swept up and piled against the Sangre de Cristo mountains.

From the 1.5-billion-year-old bedrock in the Black Canyon of the Gunnison National Monument to the 20,000-year-old eolian deposit at Great Sand Dunes National Monument, Colorado's geologic parks carry you on an immense journey not only across miles of prairie, peak, and plateau but also back through the pages of time, back from man to the dinosaur and then another giant leap backward to when the earth was almost new.

BLACK CANYON OF THE GUNNISON NATIONAL MONUMENT

Nothing along the road to the Black Canyon of the Gunnison prepares you for its empty chasm. You reach the canyon rim and there's only airy space. Dark cliffs soar, unbroken except by gullies and ledges. The distant roar of the Gunnison River drifts up to the rim as it thunders through fallen boulders far below.

Colorado's fourth-largest river, the Gunnison originates on the Continental Divide. Below the town of Gunnison, the river drops into the fifty-mile-long Black Canyon; pools behind Blue Mesa, Morrow Point, and Crystal dams for water storage, flood control, power, and recreation; and plunges into the untamed twelve-mile-long Black Canyon of the Gunnison National Monument.

The monument, a 20,763-acre park set aside in 1933, protects the canyon's deepest section. "Several western canyons exceed the Black Canyon in overall size," writes geologist Wallace Hansen. "Some are longer; some are deeper; some are narrower; and a few have walls as steep. But no other canyon in North America combines the depth, narrowness, sheerness, and somber countenance of the Black Canyon of the Gunnison."

The Gunnison River has a steep gradient, dropping 2,150 feet from the head of its canyon to its north fork junction near Delta. In this fifty miles, the Gunnison drops an average of forty-three feet per mile. That's an impressive gradient for any river, but consider this: in the two miles from Pulpit Rock to Chasm View in the monument, the river falls an astonishing 480 feet, including 180 feet in a half-mile stretch. The river's average gradient through the monument is ninety-five feet per mile. Compare that with the Green River's twelve-feet-per-mile drop in Dinosaur National Monument. That gradient, along with the abrasion of boulders rolling along the riverbed, gives the Gunnison a cutting edge.

► *The Gunnison River slices through 1.5-billion-year-old bedrock to form its dramatic Black Canyon.* GALEN ROWELL/MOUNTAIN LIGHT

► *Shadows fill the precipitous Black Canyon of the Gunnison. The canyon, here at Chasm View, reaches a depth of almost 2,000 feet.* GEORGE WUERTHNER

The Black Canyon's rock, formed between one billion and two billion years ago in an ancient mountain range, creates the canyon's mood—dark and forbidding. Composed of granite, schist, and gneiss, this rock is resistant to erosion, with the river slicing into its bed only an inch a century. The canyon is somewhere between two and three million years old.

The Black Canyon began forming 60 million years ago when today's Rocky Mountains were uplifted. Erosion tackled the mountains as they rose, with glaciers chiseling away at the peaks. The ancestral Gunnison River, laden with snowmelt, braided across a plain in western Colorado. Volcanoes in the West Elk Range north of today's canyon and in the San Juan Mountains to the south later channeled the river through a narrow valley between volcanic highlands.

Trapped in the valley, the river chewed through soft underlying volcanic rocks and sedimentary strata before carving into the bedrock beneath. By the time volcanism ceased a million years ago, the river was firmly entrenched in the bedrock. The river had nowhere to go but down. And down it went, shaping its canyon with water, rock, and time.

The canyon's rugged character also determines its life forms. Pinyon pine, juniper, and Gambel oak cover the canyon's rims. When you walk the monument's trails, you become aware of its life: a porcupine-gnawed pinyon pine; the drift of a golden eagle over the depths; a rufous-sided towhee rustling in oak leaves; the hoofbeats of an alarmed mule deer; the howls of a coyote pack. Big mammals also range into the monument—black bear, mountain lion, bighorn sheep, and elk.

The canyon's cliffs restrict life beneath the rims. White-throated swifts and cliff swallows swoop between precipices. Green islands of fir, spruce, and aspen perch on north-facing walls. Lichens work at breaking solid rock down to soil. Hawks nest in the lofty cliffs.

Tomichi, a Ute word translated as "the land of cliffs and water," is what the Ute Indians called the Black Canyon region. These nomadic hunters camped in today's park, hunting animals and gathering pinyon nuts along the canyon rims.

An 1853 railroad survey led by Captain John Gunnison first explored the river now bearing his name. After descending the upper gorge, the discouraged party climbed out, bypassing the steep canyon. Impressed by the rugged area, Gunnison noted its impracticality as a railroad route.

By the 1890s farmers had settled in the Uncompahgre Valley west of the canyon, but the meager flow of the Uncompahgre River allowed only small-scale farming. The solution seemed obvious—tap into the Gunnison River. A 1900 expedition explored the feasibility of a diversion tunnel but was a disaster. The adventurers traveled fourteen miles in three weeks through the canyon before calling it quits at a white-water torrent they called the Falls of Sorrow.

A 1901 expedition by William Torrence and A. L. Fellows completed the survey. After nine days and seventy-two river crossings, the two climbed out below today's monument boundary. Fellows wrote of their ordeal: "Our surroundings were of the wildest possible description. The roar of the water falls was constantly in our ears, and the walls of the canyon, towering half mile in

height above us, were seemingly vertical. Occasionally a rock would fall from one side or the other, with a roar and crash, exploding like a ton of dynamite when it struck bottom, making us think our last day had come." Torrence and Fellows surveyed the best sites for a diversion dam and tunnel.

By 1904 a site was picked, and work began on the six-mile-long tunnel from East Portal, just outside the monument in Curecanti National Recreation Area. Despite good pay and benefits, workers disliked the dangerous work. The average length of stay was only two weeks. Since opening in 1909, the tunnel has supplied a steady flow of water to farms in the Uncompahgre Valley.

Visitors easily explore the Black Canyon's rims today. The south rim, fifteen miles from Montrose, has a paved drive with thirteen overlooks. Chasm View is most spectacular. Sheer cliffs drop to the river 1,800 feet below, and the north rim lies a scant 1,100 feet across the void. The panorama from Dragon Point includes the Painted Wall, Colorado's highest cliff at 2,250 feet high. A visitor center at Gunnison Point details the canyon's geology, natural history, and history.

The canyon's unpaved north rim drive offers the monument's most dramatic views. At the Narrows View, rock falls straight away to the river cascading through a forty-foot gap between cliffs far below.

► *Herds of elusive bighorn sheep range through the rugged wilderness of the Black Canyon of the Gunnison National Monument.* WENDY SHATTIL/ ROBERT ROZINSKI

► *Like glowing embers the trumpet-shaped flowers of the scarlet gilia dot the hillsides and valleys of Colorado with spectacular color.* MICHAEL S. SAMPLE

Few visitors enter the canyon itself. No marked trails descend from the rims, most routes plunge down gullies to the river. One route goes down SOB Draw from the north rim. Descent takes two hours and the climb out between three and five hours. A permit is necessary to enter the canyon.

Most visitors to this wilderness world are fishermen looking for brown and rainbow trout. This stretch of the Gunnison is designated "Gold Medal Water." Fishing is by flies and lures only.

Other visitors descend the gullies to climb out the hard way—straight up. Expert climbers have ascended all the major cliffs in the monument. Some, like the Painted Wall, are multiday routes; others, like North Chasm Wall, offer excellent free climbs. A permit is required for any climbing activity.

Each time you visit the Black Canyon, nothing readies you for the impact of its deep chasm. To stand on the rim is to struggle to comprehend the earth's age and to see in the depths a picture of the last two billion years. It's the kind of place that silences idle thoughts, forcing you to dwell instead on the eternal— rock, time, and the river.

GREAT SAND DUNES NATIONAL MONUMENT

The shadows deepen in the evening light, creeping across the sand dunes. The wind has stopped blowing, and stillness envelops the dunes. Errant shafts of the setting sun tint overhead clouds pale gold and orange. Twilight's glow yields to the shades of night pulled over the eastern horizon of mountains. Among the hollows of sand are sunflowers, their yellow petals reflecting sunlight in the growing darkness. A pocket of cool air washes up from Medano Creek below, and voices from the distant campground echo across the silent vault of sand.

Great Sand Dunes National Monument, a 38,400-acre parkland established in 1932, holds the tallest dunes in the Western Hemisphere. Lying above the broad San Luis Valley in southern Colorado thirty-two miles northeast of Alamosa, sand dunes blanket 75 percent of the monument. The highest dunes rise 700 feet above the valley floor. The sand mass has a volume estimated at eight cubic miles, enough sand that it would be almost five inches deep if spread across Colorado's 103,766 square miles.

These land-locked sand dunes, swept up against the Sangre de Cristo Range, present an obvious question: "Why are they here?" Sand dunes are associated with deserts and seashores, not mountains. Since the Rockies are hardly a desert, there must be some other explanation. But the San Luis Valley, an intermountain park the size of Connecticut, receives less than ten inches of annual rainfall, making it a true desert.

The monument lies east of and in the rainshadow of the San Juan Mountains. Storms laden with moisture unload on the San Juans, and when the clouds reach the valley, all the moisture has been wrung out. Hence the San Luis Valley is Colorado's driest corner.

The dune field's birth began 20,000 years ago—only yesterday in geologic time—when ice sheets marched across North America. During that period glaciers gouged out Colorado's mountains, and snowmelt-laden rivers rushed into the valley, forming the ancestral Rio Grande. Over the next 10,000 years, a warming climate dried up the glaciers and the river. The Rio Grande, migrating west to its present course, left behind sand and silt in its old riverbed.

Centuries of wind scoured the valley floor, sweeping sand into a natural pocket below the Sangre de Cristo Range. The tumbling sand funneled toward Mosca and Medano passes, the Sangre de Cristos' low points above the dune field. There the wind, forced to rise over the mountains, dropped its load of sand. The dunes today are part of this ongoing process, for as long as the wind blows. The dune field, however, is now growing in volume rather than in size.

Wind, besides building the dunes, changes them on an almost daily basis. If

▶ *An evening thunderstorm spreads a curtain of rain across Great Sand Dunes National Monument.* PAT O'HARA

▶ *A fleet-footed pronghorn, left, the fastest North American mammal, browses on sunflowers at Great Sand Dunes.* STEWART M. GREEN

▶ *An alert gray jay, center, sits atop a tree.* STEPHEN TRIMBLE

▶ *A giant sand treader camel cricket, above, threads its way through sand ripples at Great Sand Dunes. This cricket is one of three insect species endemic to the dunes region—they live here and only here.* RANDY TRINE

you look at the dunes you will see they reflect the work of the west wind. Most are transverse dunes, meaning that the dune crest forms at a right angle to the wind's usual direction. When the wind reverses direction, blowing from the east, sand piles back onto the west side of the dunes, forming reversing dunes or "Chinese Walls." The reversing winds also hold the dunes in check, keeping them from advancing onto the mountains. The east wind pushes sand into Medano Creek where it is carried west into the valley. From there the wind recycles it onto the dunes.

The Great Sand Dunes' natural history is as intriguing as its geology. Most of the precipitation in the valley falls in summer thunderstorms. The rainshadow con-

spires with a wide temperature range, from winter's -20 degrees to summer's 90 degrees, and an elevation of 8,200 feet to make life hard for everything living on this intermountain desert.

Hiking among the dunes, you find them not nearly as lifeless as at first sight. Sunflowers spring from the sand; colonies of Indian ricegrass waver under the ripple of wind; cottonwoods, half-buried by sand, avoid suffocation by sending out new roots; beetle tracks thread across the dunes; and kangaroo rats, their burrow entrances plugged with sand during midday heat, await nightfall. Insects are among the brave that choose to live on the dunes. Three species—a circus beetle, Great Sand Dunes tiger beetle, and giant sand treader camel cricket—live only on

the Great Sand Dunes and the eastern San Luis Valley.

Most life exists along the shore of the dune sea in rabbitbrush grasslands, pinyon pine and juniper woodlands, and the riparian habitats bordering Medano and Mosca creeks. Medano Creek flows south along the eastern edge of the dune field, and Mosca Creek, originating atop the Sangre de Cristos, drops west to Medano Creek. Large mammals in the monument include mule deer, pronghorn, coyote, and bobcat. Over 150 bird species live here, with magpies, ravens, jays, hawks, and golden eagles common.

People also have lived along the dune fringe. The first inhabitants, Folsom Indian hunters, camped near springs along the dunes over 10,000 years ago.

Their campsites have yielded bison bones and fluted spear points. Later Indians, Pueblos and Utes, roamed the San Luis Valley in search of game and edible plants. Living evidence of Ute occupation of the monument grows in a ponderosa pine grove where tree bark was stripped for food during a severe winter.

The first American to see the dunes, Lieutenant Zebulon Pike, noted in his journal on January 28, 1807, "I ascended one of the largest hills of sand . . . Their appearance was exactly that of a sea in a storm (except as to color) not the least sign of vegetation existing thereon." From the highest dune Pike spied "a large river," the Rio Grande, and believed it to be the Red River, southern boundary of America's newly acquired Louisiana Purchase. Two days later, Pike and his men crossed the river, and near today's La Jara erected a stockade. Shortly afterwards, Pike was apprehended for trespassing on Spanish soil.

Now the dunes are an exhilarating playground. As former monument ranger Bob Schultz says, "The main use of the dunes is recreation. People can't wait to get out in the big cat-box." Many clamber to the highest ridges before bounding down in giant steps. Others splash in Medano Creek. If you climb the dunes, wear shoes as surface temperatures soar over 140 degrees. You can pick your own path; there are no trails across the dunes.

There are trails in other parts of the park. Montville Nature Trail (0.5 mile), historic Mosca Pass Trail (3.5 miles), and Wellington Ditch Trail (1 mile) begin near the visitor center. The Medano Pass

► *Narrowleaf cottonwoods frame the Great Sand Dunes and Medano Creek. Reaching heights of 700 feet, the dunes soar higher than any others in the Western Hemisphere.*
KENT AND DONNA DANNEN

► *The west wind exposes delicate layers of sand and snow. Volcanic rock and quartz fragments, eroded from the San Juan Range fifty miles west, compose about 80 percent of the Great Sand Dunes.*
STEPHEN TRIMBLE

Primitive Road allows jeeps to explore more backcountry, but no off-road driving on the dunes is permitted. Campers at Pinyon Flats Campground enjoy marvelous views of the dunes.

To appreciate the size of the Great Sand Dunes, it's best to walk into the dune field. Out there you can explore among the ridges and hollows of sculptured sand; you can witness the wind reshaping the graceful forms; you can watch clouds build over the mountain wall, trailing shadows across the dunes. And when you reach the top, a vast panorama spreads around you. The dune sea washes north to the peaks, and in between lies a lonely world of wind, sand, and sun.

COLORADO NATIONAL MONUMENT

The Colorado River drifts through the Grand Valley in western Colorado, meandering past cottonwood-lined banks, orchards, and towns named Palisade, Grand Junction, and Fruita. Cliffs and mountains hem the river into its valley—the Book Cliffs across the north, Grand Mesa on the east, and the Uncompahgre Plateau on the south. On the plateau's northern edge, abrupt canyons drain into the Grand Valley. These steep canyons and their precipitous rims, carved from sandstone strata draped over the plateau, form Colorado National Monument.

The 20,457-acre monument, its east entrance three miles west of Grand Junction, is a geologic feast. Every view reveals an angular architecture of mesas, buttes, buttresses, pillars, and spires. These shapes result from day-to-day erosion by wind and water.

Like Colorado's other geologic parklands, Colorado National Monument offers not only spectacular scenery but a glimpse into the earth's history. Standing on the canyon rim, you see over 1.5 billion years exposed in nine rock formations on the cliffs and slopes. The strata are neatly arranged by age, the youngest on top, the oldest at the bottom.

The monument's geologic record opens in the Precambrian era 1.5 billion years ago with the rock that now covers the canyon floors. These rocks, once

► Wingate sandstone, deposited 210 million years ago, forms distinctive cliffs and spires in Colorado National Monument, such as the Kissing Couple, left. JACK OLSON

► Below, a climber scales Independence Monument. John Otto, the park's first superintendent, made the first ascent in 1910. ED WEBSTER

► *Alongside Monument Canyon Trail, a collared lizard basks in summer sunshine.* STEPHEN TRIMBLE

thick layers of sand, silt, and mud on a sea bottom, were later deformed by heat and pressure into schist and gneiss. Molten magma injected into fissures in the rock cooled into granite.

Between the Precambrian rocks and the next layer, the Chinle Formation, over 750 million years of history are missing, erased by widespread erosion. Above the basement rocks lie eight sandstone formations—Chinle, Wingate, Kayenta, Entrada, Summerville, Morrison, Burro Canyon, and Dakota—deposited during the Mesozoic era between 210 and 150 million years ago.

The dominant rocks are the Wingate and Kayenta formations. The Wingate forms the monument's vertical cliffs. It tells a story of deserts, wind, and shifting sand. The Wingate presents evidence of a large Sahara-like dune field that once blanketed western Colorado and most of Utah. Crowned by the resistant Kayenta Formation, the Wingate is responsible for the monument's most spectacular features—Independence Monument, Pipe Organ, Kissing Couple, and the Coke Ovens.

About 70 million years ago a new uplift raised the Uncompahgre Plateau above the surrounding land. Erosion attacked the highland during the last 2 million years, when glaciers perched on the Rocky Mountains. High runoff sliced into the dipping sandstone beds on the plateau's northern end, sculpting canyons that reveal the underlying strata.

The monument's geology also shapes the lives of plants and animals. Precipitation is scarce in this rocky world, with eleven inches of annual rainfall. Temperatures range from below zero to over 100 degrees.

A pinyon pine and juniper woodland spreads across the canyon floors and climbs the ridges above the rims. Junipers prefer the canyons, while pinyons dominate the higher elevations. Sagebrush and snakewood cover the open areas, their pungent smell perfuming the air. Early summer brings color to this high desert before July's heat arrives. Flowers—Indian paintbrush, phlox, mustard, evening primrose, barrel cactus, prickly pear, and others—dot the canyon rims, and yuccas issue stalks covered with white blossoms, a favorite deer food.

The animals that live here are inconspicuous. During the heat of the day, nothing moves in the canyons. Kangaroo rats plug their burrows with sand and await evening. Deer and coyotes bed down in shrubbery or dens during the day. Bighorn sheep, reintroduced to the monument in 1979, remain aloof.

Colorado National Monument was the brainchild of one man—John Otto. It was preserved as a national monument in 1911 largely through his efforts. This trailblazer, promoter, patriot, and

▶ *Steep Wingate sandstone cliffs are topped with an erosion-resistant cap of white Kayenta sandstone in Colorado National Monument's Monument Canyon.* TOM TILL

► *Colorful exposures of the Summerville Formation lie along Colorado National Monument's Rim Rock Drive. The Summerville, laid down in a shallow sea, displays the hues of a rock rainbow.* RANDY TRINE

Drive provides the easiest way to see the canyon country today. Three short trails—Canyon Rim Trail, John Otto's Trail, and Coke Ovens Trail—skirt the canyon walls, giving dramatic views into the depths below.

Eleven other trails, covering over thirty miles, permit more exploration of the monument. Monument Canyon Trail, one of the best, drops five miles from Rim Rock Drive to the monument boundary. Another wilderness walk follows No Thoroughfare Canyon eight and a half miles from Little Park Road to Devils Kitchen. Other hikes explore untracked canyons like Red, Columbus, and Kodels.

Besides hiking and sightseeing, visitors can camp here year-round. A visitor center displays history, geology, and natural history and provides ranger-led walks and talks in summer. Cross-country skiers slide along Liberty Cap Trail after heavy snowfalls, and rock climbers scale the monument's spires.

The most popular climb is up 500-foot-high Independence Monument. John Otto made the daring first ascent in 1910 by drilling holes and inserting pipes to create a ladder to the summit. The *Grand Junction Daily News* called it "a perilous piece of work." Atop the tower Otto hoisted an American flag to celebrate Independence Day.

Colorado National Monument is a park of contrasts. While suburban Grand Junction butts against its boundary, the park preserves a slice of wilderness. Rim Rock Drive allows easy access to the monument's scenic overlooks, and narrow trails plunge into the canyons, leading to spring-fed oases, hidden alcoves full of bird song and solitude, and a geologic legacy over a billion years old.

outdoorsman settled in Monument Canyon in 1906, living in a tent below Independence Monument. In 1907 he wrote, "I came here last year and found these canyons, and they feel like the heart of the world to me. I'm going to stay and build trails and promote this place, because it should be a national park."

And build trails he did. Otto built Serpent's Trail, calling it "the crookedest road in the world" with its fifty-two switchbacks. The 2.5-mile trail still winds up a jutting peninsula of sandstone. Most hikers start the historic walk at the upper trailhead. It's all downhill that way. Otto also nurtured the dream of a Rim Rock Drive, later constructed by the Civilian Conservation Corps in the 1930s. Most of the canyons and spires retain the names Otto gave them during his twenty-one-year residence at the monument.

While early visitors were guided on horseback through Colorado National Monument, twenty-two-mile Rim Rock

DINOSAUR NATIONAL MONUMENT

► *The Green River mirrors the Park City Formation in Dinosaur National Monument.* DOUG LEE

Dinosaur National Monument bestrides the Colorado-Utah border thirty miles south of Wyoming and 295 miles west of Denver. This 211,141-acre park protects two distinct natural features: a spectacular deposit of dinosaur bones and the scenic canyon country carved by the Green and Yampa rivers.

Not surprisingly, most visitors come to view the Dinosaur Quarry. There, chipped out in bas-relief, is an extraordinary display of life buried in sandstone, a display that takes you back 140 million years to an age when reptiles ruled the earth. The story begins on August 17, 1909.

That summer paleontologist Earl Douglass searched the slopes above the Green River in northeastern Utah, and all summer he came up empty-handed. He was certain dinosaur bones lay hidden in the Morrison Formation here. Others had found fossils. Indians picked up bone fragments and carried them back to camp. John Wesley Powell noted ''reptilian remains'' when he floated past on his 1871 voyage down the Green River. In 1893 scientist O.A. Peterson discovered bones in the Morrison south of today's monument. Fifteen years later his report prompted Pittsburgh's Carnegie Museum to send Douglass to survey the Uinta Basin.

Douglass scoured the dry hillsides for four months with no luck. But sitting in a juniper's August shade, he spied a promising outcrop of sandstone on a distant hill. He scrambled over and saw, etched in a sandstone wall, the tail bones

of a giant dinosaur. Douglass wrote in his diary, ''At last in the top of the ledge where the softer overlying beds form a divide. . .I saw eight of the tail bones of a *Brontosaurus* in exact position.''

An elated Douglass extracted an almost complete seventy-foot-long skeleton, which was, at that time, the largest and most complete dinosaur ever found. With financial support from the Carnegie

▶ *The Yampa River curls around Steamboat Rock in Dinosaur's Echo Park. In 1867, Major John W. Powell named Echo Park because "Standing opposite the rock, our words are repeated with startling clearness, but in a soft, mellow tone, that transforms them into magical music."*
MELINDA BERGE/PHOTOGRAPHERS ASPEN

and *Camarasaurus.* In 1822 the most perfect skeleton ever exhumed came to light. A small *Camarasaurus,* its skull and limbs in place, made an unrivaled exhibit at the Carnegie Museum.

In 1924 quarry operations were suspended. Douglass went on to work at the University of Utah and died in 1931. Dinosaur National Monument, however, remains a tribute to Earl Douglass. He recognized the site's importance and pressed for protection. In 1915 the quarry was designated a national monument. He noted that year: "I hope that the Government. . . will uncover a large area, leave the bones and skeletons in relief and house them in. It would make one of the most astounding and instructive sights imaginable." His dream was fulfilled in 1958 when the Dinosaur Quarry building opened. Now visitors can marvel at the finest Jurassic-period dinosaur collection in the world. The quarry sits across the Utah border, seven miles north of U.S. 40.

"This quarry is the single best window in the world into the life of the dinosaurs one hundred forty million years ago," says Ann Schaffer, a member of the park's professional paleontological staff. "All the bones were deposited in a hundred-year period, so you don't see the evolution of any species. But when you look at the

Museum, Douglass built a road to the quarry, set up an office and cabin, and made the quarry his career. From 1909 to 1923, he followed the fossil bed downward. Over 350 tons of bones embedded in rock were shipped to Pittsburgh for further cleaning and analysis. Douglass discovered ten dinosaur species, including *Stegasaurus, Allosaurus, Camptosaurus, Dryosaurus,*

► *Hikers wade in sparkling Bishop Creek above Jones Hole in Dinosaur National Monument. Accessible only by river or trail, the stream is famous for its trout fishing.* STEWART M. GREEN

► *Gliding on silent Yampa River currents, rafters slide by boldly striped Tiger Wall. Iron and manganese oxide deposits streak the overhanging cliff with a thin patina of desert varnish.*
STEWART M. GREEN

quarry, it's like seeing a snapshot of Jurassic times."

Over 2,200 bones from ten different species are exposed on the quarry face. Other fossils include turtles, crocodiles, clams, trees, and mammal teeth. The monument staff has found 110 other sites with dinosaur or fossil remains in the park.

The dinosaur bones were deposited on the bends of a river that uncoiled across a wide, subtropical floodplain bordering a shallow sea to the north. Dinosaur carcasses were quickly covered by sand and gravel and preserved. Buried underground, they became time machines waiting for Earl Douglass to bring them back to the light of day.

There is much more to Dinosaur National Monument than the quarry. Out here is a wonderland chiseled out of sand-

stone. This wilderness world, designed by muddy rivers, is full of soaring amphitheaters and cliffs, shaded alcoves, sunken pockets of light and silence, and animals that appear and disappear like desert mirages.

Dinosaur is a complex "book" of rocks. Every rock layer, or formation, tells a different story, exposing bits and pieces of a drama spanning 1.3 billion years. "Dinosaur has a more complete geologic story than any other park, including the Grand Canyon," says Chief Ranger John Welch. Indeed, there are rocks here, like the billion-year-old Uinta Group, among the oldest on earth. Other strata are almost new, having been deposited within the last 20,000 years. But what makes Dinosaur unique is not just the immense time span of its rocks,

but the dramatic forms they take after folding, faulting, and erosion.

When you drive out to Harpers Corner, a tongue of rock high above the Green River, one fact becomes clear: Dinosaur's canyons are the work of relentless erosion. Four main canyons—Lodore, Whirlpool, Split Mountain, and Yampa—dissect Dinosaur's mountains, an eastern spur of the Uinta Range that rose 65 million years ago. Each canyon has a distinctive personality shaped by its rock layers and river.

T.S. Eliot once described an African river as "a strong, brown god." It's an apt description for the Yampa River. Born on the Continental Divide, the Yampa is the only natural river in the Colorado River system. It enters Dinosaur in Deerlodge Park and drops into forty-five-mile-long

► *The Fremont Indians, hunters and farmers in Dinosaur's wilderness over a thousand years ago, left outdoor galleries of rock art chiseled into sandstone cliffs. Human-like figures decorated with shields, earrings, and headdresses are common Fremont subjects.*
DAVID HISER/PHOTOGRAPHERS ASPEN

Yampa Canyon. In the upper canyon it rolls past talus slopes topped with shadowy cliffs and over short rapids like Teepee and Big Joe. Below Big Joe, the river enters its lower canyon incised in the salmon-colored Weber sandstone. Here the Yampa lazily unwinds beneath immense walls. At Horseshoe Bends it loops through seven miles of canyon to go two miles as the crow flies. The Tiger Wall, a golden hide striped with desert varnish, leans over the river on one bend.

The Yampa runs glass smooth through the bends, but ahead lies some of Colorado's most dangerous white water—Warm Springs Rapid. The rapid formed on the night of June 10, 1965, when a flash flood swept down Warm Springs Draw. The flood tumbled huge boulders into the river temporarily damming it. That night the river breached the dam and roared down its newest rapid. A few miles below Warm Springs, the Yampa is quietly lost in the Green River in Echo Park.

The Green River's somber eighteen-mile-long Lodore Canyon extends from the monument's northern boundary to Echo Park. Lodore, Dinosaur's deepest canyon, drops 3,350 feet below Zenobia Peak, the monument's high point at 9,006 feet. Lodore also holds the park's oldest rocks, Uinta Mountain quartzite, as well as some fierce rapids—Disaster Falls and Hell's Half Mile. The Green River merges with the Yampa beneath Steamboat Rock in Echo Park, a verdant pocket sandwiched by cliffs.

Below Echo Park begins ten-mile-long Whirlpool Canyon. It was described and named by Powell on his first exploration of the Green River in 1869: "The Green is greatly increased by the Yampa....All this volume of water...in a narrow channel and rushing with great velocity, is set eddying and spinning in whirlpools by projecting rocks and short curves, and the waters waltz their way through the canyon, making their own rippling, rushing, roaring music."

Split Mountain Canyon begins below Whirlpool Canyon and Island Park. It's a popular one-day run for rafters, who delight in its tumbling rapids. Moonshine Rapid, for example, is a leaping, shouting cataract that shatters to white foam and thunder. Your boat shudders through it, buckling against river boulders before rushing downstream through more rapids—S.O.B., Schoolboy, and Inglesby. After five miles of white water, the river churns you out of the canyon through a yawning mouth of cliffs that marks the end of Dinosaur's canyon country.

Rafting is a popular way to see Dinosaur's wilderness. About 12,000 visitors annually float the rivers, using a National Park Service permit system that protects the fragile rivers and canyons from being overrun. While the boating season extends from April to October, the Yampa can be run only in May and June.

Visitors can also drive into the backcountry. The thirty-one-mile-long Harpers Corner Road offers spectacular overlooks above the canyons. A one-mile trail follows the narrow neck of Harpers Corner to a stunning viewpoint 2,000 feet above the Green River. A thirteen-mile-long dirt road descends sharply from Harpers Corner Road to a campground in Echo Park.

Other roads skirt the canyon country. Four-wheel-drive Yampa Bench Road parallels Yampa Canyon for forty-six miles from Harpers Corner to Elk Springs on U.S. 40. A ten-mile dirt road off Colorado 318 gives access to the Gates of Lodore, a campground, and a nature trail. Roads penetrate Island Park, an open valley between Whirlpool and Split Mountain canyons, on Dinosaur's west end, and Deerlodge Park, the Yampa's gateway to Dinosaur, on the east.

It's easy to get into Dinosaur's backcountry. Start hiking and within a mile you'll be alone with the sagebrush, junipers, cliffs, and silence. "You can have a real wilderness experience here," Welch says. "We get few backcountry visitors, so if you go on foot you won't see anyone else out there. Over 70 percent of our visitors just go to the quarry and never see the rest of the park."

Besides displaying dinosaur bones, the quarry area offers Red Rock Nature Trail, a two-mile loop through a valley lined with flatirons of multihued sandstone. The trail introduces Dinosaur's geology and natural history. Another point of interest is the Josie Morris Cabin on Cub Creek. Josie homesteaded the land in 1914, building a log home, cultivating nearby fields, and raising chickens and cattle until her death in 1964. Along the Cub Creek Road, a self-guiding auto tour, are petroglyphs of lizards, bighorns, and human-like forms that were incised on cliffs over a thousand years ago by the Fremont Indians that inhabited the area.

Dinosaur is a refuge from civilization, a place of Indians, history, rivers, canyons, and sky. It's a place to forget the urban rat race. When you come, step out of your car and walk into the wilderness or drift down the racing current of a river. After a couple of days you'll become close to the canyon, the river, and yourself. You'll find that in Dinosaur, as in the best of wildernesses, you'll forget the outside. Nothing but the here and now exists.

► *Fossil preparator Ann Schaffer brings specimens into relief at Dinosaur Quarry, where over 2,200 bones from ten different dinosaur species lie exposed.* STEWART M. GREEN

FLORISSANT FOSSIL BEDS NATIONAL MONUMENT

Florissant Fossil Beds National Monument, fifteen miles west of Pikes Peak, is easy to pass by. Only a sign in the town of Florissant points the way south to one of Colorado's most interesting natural areas. "Florissant is famous as the valley of the fossil insects," wrote noted entomologist and nature writer Edwin Way Teale in 1960. "It was the place we wanted to see first in all of Colorado."

Hidden under Florissant's forests and meadows lies a long-ago landscape of towering sequoias and serene lakes. This prehistoric landscape is preserved in fossil form, providing glimpses of a land and time unknowable except through the imagination.

Special conditions existed at Florissant that encouraged the preservation of animals and plants, producing, in some cases, fossils unlike any others in the world. The fossils include insects like butterflies and wasps—creatures so delicate they are almost never preserved in rock—and the petrified stumps of sequoias that grew along the banks of an ancient lake.

With these fossils, Florissant found a niche in the paleontological record. An estimated 60,000 fossil specimens were unearthed here by scientists, mostly in the late nineteenth and early twentieth centuries. Now housed in museums worldwide, these specimens cover an enormous panorama of insect life. Over

▶ *A wasp leaves a delicate imprint etched in shale.* WENDY SHATTIL/ROBERT ROZINSKI

1,100 species, including examples of almost all the butterfly fossils found in North America, have been identified. Also represented are 114 plant species as well as bird, fish, and mammal species.

This singular preservation resulted from a series of volcanic events beginning some 35 million years ago. Florissant was about 2,400 to 3,000 feet above sea level at that time, or 6,100 to 5,500 feet lower than its current 8,500 feet. The climate was temperate with warm winters and hot summers, much like northeastern Mexico today. Huge sequoias lifted skyward from creek bottoms, forming forests similar to California's coast redwood groves. These giants reached heights of 250 feet and lived between 800 and 1,200 years. Ferns and shrubs thrived beneath the trees.

This scene was disrupted, however, by eruptions of the Thirtynine Mile Volcanic Field west of the monument. For 500,000 years volcanism altered and redirected the region's creeks, ponding them into shallow lakes, including twelve-mile-long Lake Florissant. Long intervals between eruptions allowed lakeside and aquatic ecosystems to reestablish themselves.

One theory is that one violent episode was similar to the 1980 Mount St. Helens eruption. Shock waves from the explosion blew the tops off sequoias, while mudflows buried their stumps with fifteen feet of hot mud, cinders, ash, and water. The wood of the buried trees became petrified, replicating their beauty and strength in stone.

Volcanism also preserved plant, insect, and animal remains in Lake Florissant. A pattern of eruptions followed by years of peace led to the gradual buildup of lake-bottom sediments. Paper-thin ash and silt layers accumulated, reflecting each cyclic volcanic event. Insects and leaves were deposited in the sediments by wind, falling ash, and spring runoff. Eventually the lake filled with sediment, dried up, and was capped with a final mudflow that entombed a nearly complete ecosystem.

Over millions of years, the burden of

► Only the petrified stump remains of a giant Sequoia affinis *that once grew along the banks of an ancient lake in today's Florissant Fossil Beds.*
STEVE MULLIGAN

► *Florissant visitors marvel at the Trio, a group of sequoias that grew from a common root system.*
STEWART M. GREEN

T.D.A. Cockerell began working the beds in 1906. Some of his finds included four species of tsetse fly (the dreaded African carrier of sleeping sickness) and many fossil butterflies.

After the paleontologists came the souvenir hunters. The private fossil beds became a tourist attraction with fees charged for both looking and digging. For fifty years an untold amount of petrified Wood and fossils exited in the pockets of tourists. In the 1960s a housing subdivision threatened the fossil beds, but a grassroots effort by residents stopped the development and prevented the loss of irreplaceable information. In 1969 the National Park Service acquired 5,992 acres, protecting the ancient lakebed and its underground wealth as Florissant Fossil Beds National Monument.

The monument, thirty-five miles west of Colorado Springs, is growing in popularity. Florissant saw 127,000 visitors in 1986, a startling rise over 1984's 55,000. The monument is a day-use-only park offering outdoor recreation including hiking, cross-country skiing, and wildlife study. Year-round educational programs detail the monument's geology, natural history, and history.

Almost eleven miles of trails cross Florissant. The half-mile, self-guided Walk Through Time Trail introduces visitors to the monument's fossils, including the Trio (three sequoias that grew from a common root system). The Petrified Forest Loop leads to the Big Stump, the largest known *Sequoia affinis* with a 13-foot diameter and 41.9-foot circumference. The 2.1-mile Sawmill Trail traverses hillsides cloaked in pine, spruce, and fir, crosses meadows where deer and elk graze, threads through a quaking aspen grove, and follows a ridge

sediments etched delicate imprints of life in the shale. So detailed are the fossils in this mountain Pompeii that exquisite impressions of the tiniest insects—mosquitoes, gnats, and even lice—are preserved.

The Florissant Fossil Beds lay undisturbed until officially discovered in 1873 by Dr. A.C. Peale of the Hayden Survey. Although the area was known to settlers and Indians, Peale is credited with the first scientific investigation of the fossil beds. He wrote in his report:

"About one mile south of Florissant, at the base of a small hill of sandstone, capped with conglomerate, are twenty or thirty stumps of silicified wood. This locality has been called 'Petrified Stumps' by the people in the vicinity."

Other paleontologists followed Peale. Dr. Samuel Scudder exhumed 1,144 fossil insect species from Florissant. The most numerous insects he uncovered were ants, collecting 4,000 specimens of fifty different species. English entomologist

that offers views of Pikes Peak.

Visitors also explore Florissant's recent history at the Hornbek Homestead. Settled by Adeline Hornbek and her two sons and daughter in 1878, the homestead preserves their original house as well as a carriage house, root cellar, and barn. The Hornbeks raised cattle and cut hay in the meadows.

Florissant is an outdoor museum, full of exhibits depicting life and its long history. We can find the ancient past in its ash deposits and recreate the glory of what was once here in our mind's eye. Or we can look across this mountain parkland and redefine our own world.

► *Eastern saddle-notch joints, not requiring nails or wooden pegs, join corner logs at Florissant's Hornbek Homestead, left.* MICHAEL S. SAMPLE

► *The 1878 homestead of Adeline Hornbek and her children, right, has been restored by the National Park Service to interpret the area's early ranch life.* STEWART M. GREEN

► Bright note of summer cheer, a red columbine flares along a moist forest edge. Red columbine grows in subalpine forests west of the Continental Divide in Colorado, Utah, and New Mexico. MICHAEL S. SAMPLE

ROXBOROUGH STATE PARK

Imagine Colorado 150 years ago—only sun and silence, Indian pathways, towering rocks unmarred by graffiti, no roads or automobiles, no knick-knack shops. Well, you don't have to imagine anymore. That's Roxborough State Park today.

Roxborough, a 1,598-acre park fifteen miles southwest of Denver, opened its gates in 1987. Previously, Roxborough was privately held, although as early as 1910 both Colorado and Denver made efforts to acquire it as a park. Denver mayor Robert Speer said in 1910 that Roxborough "should be owned by the city for the free use of the people." The city was unable to raise $6,000 to purchase the area. Other efforts met with defeat, and the land was sold in 1967 to the Woodmoor Corporation, which planned a housing development. But in 1975 Woodmoor went bankrupt, and the State of Colorado was able to buy 500 acres. Subsequent land purchases brought the park acreage to today's 1,598. Roxborough became a state park in 1975, but access problems delayed its opening until 1987.

These difficulties, however, saved the park from overuse. "If it had been bought years ago, Roxborough would have been heavily developed," says Park Manager Susan Trumble. "We were able to look closely at parks developed for the drive-through experience like Garden of the Gods outside Colorado Springs, and we felt this park should be different. So we planned for quiet activities. It's not a glitzy park; instead it's a tranquil place to hike, study nature, and enjoy the scenery."

And Roxborough's scenery is, indeed, marvelous. The park preserves a series of sandstone hogbacks. The resistant layers—the Fountain Formation, Lyons sandstone, and Dakota Formation—stand in long rows before the abrupt Front Range mountains. The Fountain Formation, forming the most prominent hogbacks, was deposited 300 million years ago as coarse sediments swept off the Ancestral Rockies. In the alternating strata, you see a history of streambeds, some laden with boulders, cobbles, and pebbles, others with sand and silt. The iron-rich rock ranges in hue from chocolate to rose.

Shallow valleys between the ridges teem with life. Roxborough, a meeting place for plants and animals from both mountain and prairie, boasts nine distinct

► *Spires and slabs of 300-million-year-old Fountain Formation sandstone tower over grassy meadows and Gambel oak in Roxborough State Park.*
STEWART M. GREEN

► *Cross-country skiers skim across fresh snow in Roxborough State Park.*
W. PERRY CONWAY

plant communities. Forests of Gambel oak, some as tall as forty feet, crowd the hillsides. Meadows are a tangle of grasses and, where they flatten, become a mass of sedges and reeds. Wildflowers are scattered across the park—wallflowers and golden banner on the oak forest edge, fields of mustard, salsify, lupine, and penstemon in the open. Ponderosa pine and Douglas fir thrive on moist slopes, both well below their normal elevation. Other high-country strangers include quaking aspen. "Aspens," says Park Naturalist Vicky Trammel, "are very rare at this elevation, 6,200 feet."

The aspens might be a relict stand left over from the last ice age when the climate was cooler.

Roxborough, with elevations ranging from 5,900 feet by the park entrance to 7,200 feet at the top of Carpenter Peak, is home to many animals, including coyote, red fox, porcupine, raccoon, weasels, bobcats, and mule deer. An elk herd on Carpenter Peak ranges into the park, along with black bear and mountain lion. One hundred twelve bird species have been identified here, including nesting golden eagles. Common snakes are prairie rattlesnake, bullsnake, and yellow-bellied racers.

Three trails explore the park's valleys. The most popular is 2.5-mile-long Fountain Valley Trail. Lined with towering slabs, it follows Fountain Valley north to the ruins of the historic Persse Place, a 1901 homestead, then loops back along the Dakota Hogback to the visitor center. The one-mile-long Willow Creek Trail introduces Roxborough's plant communities. Four-mile-long Carpenter Peak Trail provides breathtaking views of the park below and beyond to downtown Denver. Hiking is allowed only on designated trails, and absolutely no climbing is permitted.

Roxborough State Park has significant prehistoric treasures. An archaeological survey revealed over forty prehistoric sites, primarily campsites, quarry stations, and work areas, with evidence of human occupation over the last 5,000 years. Roxborough was designated a National Archaeological District in 1983 for the antiquity of these discoveries.

Besides being an archaeological district, Roxborough has been designated a State Natural Area by the Colorado Division of Natural Resources and a National Natural Landmark by the National Park Service for its diverse ecosystems and spectacular rock formations.

Today, Roxborough is threatened by development. Subdivisions, creeping south, already threaten Roxborough. But Trumble vows, "This won't become a city park for Denver. This won't be a park with all things for all people. Roxborough is unique, so we're very protective of what we have here." With sentiments like that, Roxborough should remain an enclave of wildness and natural diversity for many years to come.

ELDORADO CANYON STATE PARK

Like conquistadors searching for the legendary El Dorado, rock climbers today probe the rock walls of Eldorado Canyon for personal rewards. An awesome gash cut by South Boulder Creek as it races from the Continental Divide to the plains seven miles south of Boulder, the canyon is protected in 848-acre Eldorado Canyon State Park. "Eldorado Canyon is a spectacular state park," says Senior Ranger Bob Toll, "and it's one of the few canyons west of Denver that doesn't have a highway up it."

Angular cliffs, varying in color from gold and rust red to ebony black and gray, pierce the canyon's skyline. Redgarden Wall, the tallest cliff, towers 850 feet above the rushing creek. Other cliffs like West Ridge and Hawk-Eagle Ridge are upturned sandstone bands that climb the craggy slopes of Shirttail Peak.

Eldorado's cliffs eroded out of the Fountain Formation, a 300-million-year-old layer of sandstone, siltstone, and conglomerate deposited along the eastern edge of the Ancestral Rockies. About 65 million years ago, as today's Rockies rose, the Fountain Formation was dragged upward into tilted ridges along the mountain edge. Erosion by creeks stripped away softer rocks, gouging canyons and leaving cliffs on the mountains above the plains.

The chief architect of Eldorado Canyon then, like Colorado's other canyon parklands, is water, tumbling streams filled with snowmelt from the high country. Sit beside South Boulder Creek in June and you can hear the sounds of erosion—the thunder of white water and the rumble of boulders grinding along the creekbed. The result: a vertical topography filled with amphitheaters, buttresses, temples, and pyramids—the rock landscape of Eldorado Canyon.

This landscape brings climbers. "Eldorado Canyon, along with the Shawangunks in New York and Yosemite Valley in California, is one of the three best climbing areas in the United States," says climbing writer Ed Webster. "Every year climbers from every continent come to climb at Eldorado." They come to test their skill and nerve on over 2,000 different routes. Most come to ascend the classic routes—Bastille Crack, Wind Ridge, the Naked Edge, Ruper, Grand Giraffe, and the Yellow Spur.

About 70 percent of Eldorado's 180,000 annual visitors come to climb; the rest sightsee, watch the climbers, picnic, and hike on three trails. Two short trails—Rattlesnake Gulch Trail and Streamside Trail—offer scenic views and hiking in the inner canyon. The third, the strenuous 5.5-mile Eldorado Canyon Trail, begins by the ranger station at the park's western edge and climbs up to the Crescent Meadows section of the park.

West of the lower canyon lies private property, but above it stretches Crescent Meadows, a detached unit of Eldorado

► *South Boulder Creek cascades over its bed in Eldorado Canyon. The swift creek, filled with meltwater, gouged out the rugged canyon over the last million years.*
GEORGE WUERTHNER

► *Dwarfed by the vertical architecture, rock climbers scale the West Buttress of the Bastille. Climbers throughout the world recognize Eldorado Canyon as a premier rock gymnasium.* JOE ARNOLD JR.

Canyon State Park. The meadows, distinct from Eldorado's rugged canyon, are covered with grass and forests. This area is undeveloped, but plans include a visitor center, trails, and campground.

The Colorado Division of Parks and Outdoor Recreation hopes to increase Eldorado's size further. A parcel they want to acquire is the Mickey Maus, a rock formation south of Eldorado Canyon. The Mickey Maus is threatened by the proposed expansion of a quarry that would eventually extend from the mountain base to summit, all within sight and sound of the state park. "We're against the mining," says Ranger Toll. "It will be a visual eyesore; the blasting could alter the stability of the park's rocks; we're concerned for visitor safety on Highway 170 from the increase in truck traffic; and there will be dust pollution." Toll is confident that the Mickey Maus will be part of the park in the future.

Before Eldorado Canyon became a state park in 1978, it had a storied past. The small town of Eldorado Springs below the canyon sprang up as a fashionable resort in the early twentieth century around a 76-degree hot spring. Three thermal pools, a dance hall, and plush hotels lured visitors. Its most famous honeymooners were Ike and Mamie Eisenhower in 1915.

But what most early Boulder residents remember about Eldorado Canyon is Ivy Baldwin and his "swinging wire." Between 1906 and 1949 Baldwin, a stuntman, wirewalker, balloonist, and parachutist, walked a high wire strung 300 feet above South Boulder Creek eighty-nine times. During his first walk he stood on his head. He knelt midway on his last walk in 1949, on his eighty-second birthday, acknowledging the applause of 3,000 spectators.

Baldwin's spirit of adventure lives on in the climbers who search Eldorado's heights for their pot of gold. They find it, too, high on the cliffs where the only sound is the wind's moan, and the only feeling is the soaring freedom of an eagle.

GARDEN OF THE GODS

The Garden of the Gods, west of Colorado Springs, excites the senses. It's a dramatic landscape, a symphony in stone. Here, below Pikes Peak, the Garden nestles in a valley, its monuments arranged like an outdoor sculpture garden. The bizarre rocks tease the imagination into seeing fanciful shapes, reflected by the rock names—Three Graces, Steamboat Rock, Kissing Camels, and Weeping Indian. The Garden of the Gods, a Colorado Springs city park since 1910, has awed and inspired generations of visitors, beginning with the Ute Indians who camped among the red rocks.

After Colorado Springs was founded in 1871, the Garden of the Gods became a popular tourist destination. Nineteenth century travel writers touted the Garden as one of the West's scenic wonders. In 1885 *New York Tribune* correspondent Ernest Ingersoll described the rocks as "fanciful images of things seen and unseen, which stand thickly over hundreds of acres like mouldering ruins of some half-buried city of the desert." *Collier's Weekly* reporter Julian Street called it a "a pale, pink joke." Famed writer and poet Helen Hunt Jackson wrote, "You wind among rocks of every conceivable and inconceivable shape and size...all bright red, all motionless and silent, with a strange look of having been just stopped and held back in the very climax of some supernatural catastrophe."

There's nothing supernatural, however, about the Garden of the Gods. The rocks are a series of once-horizontal sedimentary layers tilted upwards by the rising Rocky Mountains, 65 million years ago. The sandstone strata, deposited between 70 and 300 million years ago, were heaved, twisted, churned, and faulted into stubby ridges that paralleled the mountains. As the layers rose, wind and water attacked the rock. Softer stone was worn away to valleys, while resistant layers were left standing as hogbacks.

Few Colorado parks can boast the variety of rock types and ages found in the Garden. The formations range from billion-year-old Pikes Peak granite to gravel deposited within the last 10,000 years. Other rocks include the 4,000-foot-thick Fountain Formation, the alluvial remains of mountains that rose here 300 million years ago, and Lyons sandstone, forming the Gateway Rocks, which was laid down as sand dunes.

Besides being a lesson in geology, the Garden of the Gods is a biological melting pot, an area where life zones from prairie and mountain intertwine. The Garden's dominant ecosystem—the pinyon pine and juniper woodland—creeps across

rocky slopes. Botanists estimate some of the Garden's oldest junipers are over 1,000 years old. Thickets of Gambel oak fill the valleys, harboring pasqueflowers, penstemon, and Indian paintbrush in their shade. Ponderosa pine and Douglas fir intrude onto the Garden's upper ridges.

The Garden of the Gods is hardly a wildlife refuge, with Colorado Springs edging the park's boundary. The animals living here are shy, secretive, or nocturnal—raccoons, porcupines, deer mice, squirrels, and mule deer. Freezing winter weather occasionally drives bighorn sheep and mountain lion into the park.

More than anything else, the Garden of the Gods is a park for people. A place to escape the city, to meditate and walk among the cathedral-like rocks. A road

► *Balanced Rock, poised above a meditative visitor, is one of the Garden of the Gods' most famous attractions.* STEWART M. GREEN

► *Sunset fills the Garden of the Gods with a fiery blaze of color. Flier Charles Lindbergh, describing a 1916 visit, wrote, "I think I have never seen a more spectacular and magnificent place."*
SPENCER SWANGER/TOM STACK & ASSOCIATES

system loops through the park, allowing easy access to the major formations, Balanced Rock, and Spring Canyon.

Balanced Rock, weighing some 300 tons, rests delicately above the road. Visitors pose beneath this geologic oddity, arms outstretched as if holding the massive boulder in place. Until 1932 the rock was privately owned by Balanced Rock Scenic Attractions. The owner erected a wall around the rock and charged tourists to see the marvel.

Hikers have lots of trails to follow in the Garden of the Gods. The most popular is the paved trail that threads through oak groves below South Gateway Rock, Montezuma's Tower, and the Three Graces. Another trail contours across steep slopes west of the rocks, giving views of the Garden and the city beyond. Other visitor uses include an annual ten-kilometer race, an Easter sunrise service, and rock climbing. While 1.7 million visitors crowd through the park each year, only 800 climbers attempt its cliffs. Over 150 routes of varying difficulty ascend the formations.

Ever since the heirs of Charles Elliott Perkins gave the Garden of the Gods to Colorado Springs in 1910 as "a public resort free to all the world," visitors have flocked to the 1,368-acre park. Despite urban pressures, the Garden of the Gods remains a special place. In early morning, color washes the park—the sandstone reddens with the rising sun and the snowy bulk of Pikes Peak is etched against a flawless sky. In the morning quiet, the Garden teaches its final geology lesson: that life, measured against unfathomable rock and endless time, is a momentary way station on earth's immense journey through space.

► *A paved pathway encircles Montezuma's Tower, left, in the Garden of the Gods. Along with the other formations, these rocks are erosion-resistant remnants of ancient sandstone.*
MELINDA BERGE/PHOTOGRAPHERS ASPEN

► *Stepping across an airy gap, a rock climber stretches for the summit of the Three Graces. The Garden of the Gods saw Colorado's earliest technical climbing with Albert Ellingwood's pioneering ascents in the 1920s.* STEWART M. GREEN

ROYAL GORGE

The Arkansas River leaves the Colorado Rockies in a big way. After dropping 6,000 feet from its headwaters above Leadville, it slices through a block of 1.5-billion-year-old rock, forming the Royal Gorge. Eight miles long, 1,250 feet deep, and lined with pink walls, the chasm funnels the Arkansas down steep chutes. Its currents pound over boulders in one last mad fling before draining quietly into the broad valley below Canon City. The Royal Gorge, twelve miles west of Canon City, is preserved in a 5,120-acre park by Canon City.

How the Gorge formed is an intriguing story. "What you have here," says geologist Sue Raabe, who has studied, analyzed, and walked the Royal Gorge region for years, "is a fifty-square-mile fault block that was uplifted, tilted, and rotated by ancient faults from 70 million years ago. The rocks, responding to pressure by the faults, popped up." The actual popping up happened during the final uplift of today's Rocky Mountains some 6 to 7 million years ago.

Continued uplift further rotated and squeezed the fault block, forming a ridge down its midsection. Water erosion attacked weak spots in the ridge, developing stream drainages down either side. The west-flowing stream ran toward the ancestral Arkansas River near Salida, and the east-flowing one toward Canon City. The next step was a classic case of "stream piracy." The creek with the steepest drainage, hence the greater erosive power, pirated the flow of the other creek. In this case, the east-flowing

► *A mosaic of lichens clings to a boulder on the rim of the Royal Gorge. Lichens, a partnership between fungi and algae, work at the humble task of breaking solid rock down to soil. Lichens are among the world's oldest living organisms.* STEWART M. GREEN

stream captured the west-flowing one in the Royal Gorge.

By a million years ago the stage was set for the final act in the gorge's formation. Increased runoff during glacial periods in the mountains gave the Arkansas more erosive strength than it has now, and the river carved into the gneiss, schist, and granite bedrock of the Gorge with ice-age meltwater. The Arkansas still slices into its floor, although the river's cutting

power is lessened by upstream dams that divert its water to Front Range cities. Raabe estimates that the Royal Gorge is deepening about a tenth of an inch every century.

The Royal Gorge is a geologic marvel. Its canyon has long attracted visitors who gaze into it from Inspiration Point and Point Sublime. During the late nineteenth century the Gorge was a famed tourist attraction. Helen Hunt Jackson, a

Colorado Springs poet, wrote, "From the moment when you first reach the top of the grand amphitheater-like plateau in which the rift was made until the moment in which you stand on the very edge of the chasm and look dizzily over and down, there is but one thought, but one sense—the thought of wonder, the sense of awe."

The Gorge's most celebrated historic incident culminated a four-year scrap between the Atchison, Topeka and Santa Fe Railroad and the Denver & Rio Grande Railroad. Through the 1870s both lines pushed into the Colorado Rockies in search of lucrative freight markets.

In 1879 the lines saw opportunity beckoning at Leadville where silver mines promised a bonanza to the first railroad to reach it. The easiest rail line followed the pathway carved by the Arkansas River. Both railroads began laying track toward the Royal Gorge. Each railroad also formed private armies to harass the opposition. Bridges were burned, survey stakes pulled up, and railbeds buried under rock avalanches. A settlement finally gave the Denver & Rio Grande the gorge route, while the Santa Fe took a route to New Mexico. The railroad still traverses the canyon bottom, which is, in places, so narrow the railbed hangs over the river.

Canon City acquired the Royal Gorge in 1906 after the Canon City Businessmen's Association lobbied for the park to cash in on the tourist trade. Their efforts paid off when Congress ceded 5,120 acres "for the use and benefit of the public."

Today Canon City leases 640 acres of Royal Gorge Park to the private Royal Gorge Company, which pays the city a handsome percentage of its revenues

▶ *The highest suspension bridge in the world spans the shadowy Royal Gorge. Built in 1928 by a Texas promoter, the bridge stands 1,053 feet above the Arkansas River. The bridge is the centerpiece of a largely primitive park owned by Canon City.* ED COOPER

▶ *Green boughs adorn a Rocky Mountain juniper. Preferring dry, rocky slopes, junipers dominate Colorado's geologic parklands.*

W. PERRY CONWAY

generated by sales, tolls, and admissions. The city garners about a half million dollars annually, with most of the money used for lowering property taxes.

The Royal Gorge features the world's highest suspension bridge, measuring 1,053 feet from the bridge to the river. In 1928 Lon P. Piper, a toll bridge promoter from Texas, proposed a gorge bridge to Canon City. The city agreed to his proposal, and work on the $350,000 bridge began immediately. After the bridge opened in 1929, the Canon City *Daily Record* wrote, "The Royal Gorge bridge does not profane nor vandalize the grandeur and sublimity of the great chasm it spans, but adds to its beauty."

The gorge is a tourist attraction, a place for visitors to marvel at both nature's and man's handiwork. Most walk across the bridge, stopping to peer down at the foaming thread of river below. Some descend the world's steepest incline railway to the canyon bottom. Others ride in cable cars strung across an airy half mile of canyon. A few prefer walking away from the bridge, to sit on the canyon rim among the junipers. Fewer still penetrate the gorge itself. Those who do find thrills on some of Colorado's most dangerous white water by rafting or kayaking through the canyon. The Arkansas River boasts eight miles of almost continuous rapids, including notorious Sunshine Falls, the gorge's largest rapid.

"Most people don't realize," says Canon City Park Superintendent John Nichols, "that almost all of the Royal Gorge is a primitive area." In contrast to the developed section of the canyon, the rest of the park is untouched. The city runs a primitive campground, and a number of unmarked trails stop at canyon overlooks, offering views into the gorge.

No matter how you see the Royal Gorge, by rim or river, watch long enough and you'll find one of those priceless moments that stays with you forever. Sunset gilds the mountains around the canyon; wind whispers through a juniper; the river roar echoes off the walls like the sound of a freight train; a summer storm drops a curtain of rain over the rim. Standing there, you'll be inclined to say, as Bob Hope did on his first visit, "Golly, what a gully!'

TEMPLE CANYON AND RED CANYON PARKS

Canon City also owns two other geologic parklands—Temple Canyon and Red Canyon parks. Both are primitive and largely unknown. Superintendent John Nichols says, "The parks are used mostly by people from Canon City as well as Colorado Springs and Pueblo. But not too many people outside the area really know about them.''

Red Canyon, a 600-acre park ten miles north of Canon City, is secluded by rough mountains and hidden from nearby highways. It's a jumble of upturned sandstone layers along a base of mountains. The sweeping strata of the Fountain Formation here tells the story of torrential streams and rivers draining east off Frontrangia some 300 million years ago. Water is Red Canyon's primary erosive agent. Quick runoff from thunderstorms scours the creekbeds, undercutting cliffs and deepening canyons. Winter water, alternately freezing and thawing, chips out sandstone pieces. Details of erosion's deft handiwork abound at Red Canyon Park. A window perches atop a rock fin; a spire leans crazily into the wind; a boulder balances on a cliff edge.

Many animals roam the pinyon pine and juniper forest that covers Red Canyon Park. Jays, crows, and magpies perch atop silvered junipers. Mule deer clatter across sandstone pavement. Mountain lion, bobcat, coyote, and bear frequent the surrounding wildland.

The park is primitive. A dirt road twists past the main rock formations and a small picnic and camping area invites visitors. The park offers hiking, but there are no trails—you find your own path.

Temple Canyon Park is hidden behind mountains six miles west of Canon City. It's an unfinished landscape carved by Grape Creek as it turns northeast at the foot of the Wet Mountains. The 800-foot-deep canyon, carved over the last million years, follows faults in the bedrock along the southern edge of the uplifted fault block split by the Royal Gorge.

The Indian Temple, for which the canyon is named, is a concave amphitheater tucked into a cliff above the creek. A supposed duel between the chiefs of the Ute and Blackfoot tribes over an Indian maiden took place here. No evidence, however, substantiates the myth. Arrowheads and petroglyphs in the

► *Time and water whittle a spire in Red Canyon Park north of Canon City.* STEWART M. GREEN

► *Grape Creek slices through rugged Temple Canyon Park. Owned by Canon City, the park offers primitive hiking, camping, and fishing.* STEWART M. GREEN

park indicate Indians did know of the canyon. A narrow gauge railroad from Canon City to Westcliffe passed through the canyon. One passenger noted in 1911, "The canyon is beyond question the most beautiful in marvelous coloring, wondrous splendor of foliage, picturesque cascades and winding streams of any in Colorado." Nothing remains of the railroad's passage.

A rough dirt road threads along the southern edge of the 640-acre park. A picnic and camping area is perched on the south canyon rim. If you walk out past the tables to the rocky heights, Temple Canyon drops away precipitously. Standing on its rim, among shattered boulders and twisted pinyon, you feel alone—the canyon walls block out the rest of the world. ■

► *Abert's squirrels prefer ponderosa pine forests for food, cover, and nesting. Not storing food for the winter like other tree squirrels, they feed on the inner bark of twigs. Pine cones are their preferred summer food.* WENDY SHATTIL/ROBERT ROZINSKI

Every park is a refuge.
—ENOS MILLS

ISLANDS OF LIFE

ECOLOGICAL
PARKS

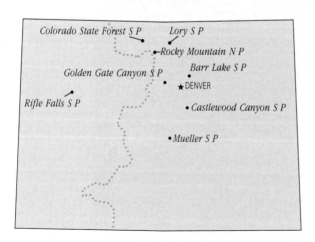

Almost all of Colorado's parklands are, in one way or another, ecological parks. Each preserves a part of what was once wilderness, a land of mountains, forests, and prairies, a land full of animals and birds, a land of plenty. Colorado's Indians—Arapahoe, Kiowa, Ute, and Anasazi—revered this abundant land. They saw its resources, the relationships of plants, animals, and people. They observed how climate and precipitation could throw life out of its natural order. They understood the fragile balance between feast and famine.

The coming of Europeans marked the end of that Colorado wilderness. Forests were harvested, prairies were plowed, rivers were harnessed, and mountains were mined. Wilderness contained nothing that society could value. The land was, and still is, a commodity to be bought and sold.

If you look at Colorado's wilderness now, you see that it survives only in isolated pockets of parkland. Many of these parks are islands, like Lory State Park near Fort Collins and Roxborough and Barr Lake state parks on the outskirts of the Denver metro area, awash in a sea of encroaching development and growing population. Some, like Mueller, Rifle Falls, Golden Gate Canyon, and Castlewood Canyon state parks, protect unique environments as well as provide outdoor opportunities for Coloradans. Others are large tracts of wild lands with pristine ecosystems such as Rocky Mountain National Park and Colorado State Forest State Park.

Whereas every park is an ecological island, each of these parklands was specifically created, to protect unique natural areas or ecosystems. Each is a window in time, allowing us to see, interpret, and understand the natural beauty and ecological diversity of Colorado.

► *A sunny close-up of a wild rose.* MICHAEL S. SAMPLE

► *A herd of elk grazes across a wide meadow in Rocky Mountain National Park. Beyond towers the 14,255-foot summit of Longs Peak.* WENDY SHATTIL/ROBERT ROZINSKI

ROCKY MOUNTAIN NATIONAL PARK

► *An aerial view reveals the dramatic glacier-carved face of Longs Peak. Indians are rumored to have set eagle traps atop its flat summit, but the first recorded ascent was in 1868. Over 7,000 climbers now scale the peak annually.* W. PERRY CONWAY

Along the Continental Divide in northern Colorado a spectacular collection of peaks is assembled in Rocky Mountain National Park. This 265,193-acre park, Colorado's largest, boasts 113 named peaks over 10,000 feet, 76 topping 12,000 feet, 19 over 13,000 feet, and 1 over 14,000 feet. Longs Peak, Colorado's fifteenth highest peak, is the park's highest point at 14,255 feet.

The divide separates the Atlantic and Pacific watersheds and splits the park in half. Rows of jagged mountains march down the divide, with two subsidiary ranges—the Never Summer Mountains and the Mummy Range—breaking off in the northwest. The eastern slope gives birth to the Cache la Poudre, Big Thompson, and St. Vrain rivers. The Colorado River, its headwaters at La Poudre Pass, drains the western slope. The divide is also an effective barrier to travelers. Indeed, only Trail Ridge Road, the nation's highest continuous paved highway, traverses the park's mountain crest, and only Bear Lake and Old Fall River roads penetrate the park's interior.

Rocky Mountain is Colorado's most popular park. Visitation averages over 2.5 million annually. Established in 1915 as America's tenth national park, it protects pristine mountain ecosystems. Naturalist and writer Enos Mills, who led the campaign for the park, described them in 1909: "The region is almost entirely above the altitude of 7,500 feet, and in it are forests, streams, waterfalls, snowy peaks, great canyons, glaciers, scores of species of wild birds, and more than a thousand varieties of wildflowers."

The alpine zone, the land above the trees, is Rocky Mountain's most noticeable ecosystem. One third of the

► Cross-country skiers, far left, break tracks through a subalpine forest below Pilot Mountain and 13,310-foot Mount Alice in Rocky Mountain National Park's Wild Basin. The park offers 350 miles of trails for hikers and skiers.
JOE ARNOLD JR.

► Inching across a steep icefield, a climber, left, ascends the east face of Thatchtop above Glacier Gorge. Rocky Mountain, recognized for its technical climbing, boasts 113 named peaks above 10,000 feet.
ED WEBSTER

park lies above treeline, which occurs between 11,000 and 11,400 feet. The rest of the park is a patchwork of spruce, fir, and pine woodlands broken by wide meadows.

To see Rocky Mountain's diverse life zones, drive thirty-seven miles along Trail Ridge Road. In less than ten miles the road climbs 5,000 feet from ponderosa pine woodlands near Estes Park to alpine tundra at its highest point of 12,183 feet.

Following an old Ute Indian trail, Trail Ridge Road runs above treeline for eleven miles and over 12,000 feet for 2.5 miles. It provides a rare opportunity to study and observe the alpine tundra zone, where winter is either in force or just around the corner.

During summer's six-to-eight-week growing season, the tundra is a colorful mass of wildflowers. Botanists estimate that some 250 plant species grow above

treeline in the Rockies, while another 100 occur both above and below treeline.

The flora hugs the ground in dense mats to mitigate the severe climate of the mountains. In the high winds (one researcher clocked summer winds on Trail Ridge at 174 miles per hour), dry air, low soil moisture, and fierce sunlight, plants must adapt to survive. Most tundra plants are perennial—one summer is too short for them to complete their life

► *Hikers take a break beside Paul Bunyan's Boot, above, on Rocky Mountain's Lumpy Ridge.*
KENT AND DONNA DANNEN

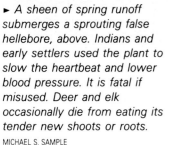

► *A sheen of spring runoff submerges a sprouting false hellebore, above. Indians and early settlers used the plant to slow the heartbeat and lower blood pressure. It is fatal if misused. Deer and elk occasionally die from eating its tender new shoots or roots.*
MICHAEL S. SAMPLE

cycles. Some are long lived, adding only a few leaves each year. Alpine phlox, for instance, can grow for as long as 150 years. Other alpine plants include lichens and mosses that cover exposed rocks.

Treeline marks the highest elevation at which trees can live. Enos Mills called it "the line of battle between the woods and the weather." Wind-blasted stands of spruce and fir, called *krummholz* (German for "crooked wood"), form miniature forests along the treeline. Tree growth is slow in the low temperatures, harsh winds, and short growing season. A 200-year-old krumm-

holz tree might be only four inches in diameter and four feet tall.

Few animals inhabit the tundra zone. The white-tailed ptarmigan lives here year-round, becoming white in winter and mottled brown in summer. Common mammals include the marmot, a burrowing rodent, and pika, a relative of the rabbit. Mule deer, elk, and bighorn sheep range across the tundra, while mountain lion, bobcat, black bear, coyote, and fox are occasional visitors.

Rocky Mountain's alpine zone is extremely susceptible to human damage. Ecologists estimate that it takes from 400

to 1,000 years for a trampled tundra area to restore itself. Park administrators curtail human use of the tundra by providing paved walkways along Trail Ridge Road, establishing "tundra protection areas," fencing delicate areas, and restoring vegetation by transplanting native plants. "We try to educate people to the fragility of tundra," says Chief Park Naturalist Glen Kaye. "An army of rangers can't keep people off it, but once they recognize their impact, they keep off it themselves."

High visitation affects more than the tundra—it affects every visitor's

► *Common residents of Rocky Mountain's alpine tundra life zone, yellow-bellied marmots frolic along Trail Ridge Road. Marmots, also known as whistle-pigs for their loud chirps, survive by feeding mainly on alpine meadow grass. Thick stores of fat fortify them during their long winter sleep.*
W. PERRY CONWAY

experience. On a busy summer day as many as 30,000 people can be spread across the park, and it can accommodate a summer overnight population of 5,000, including backcountry campsites. Backcountry overnight use, however, has dropped dramatically from a high of 62,000 in the late 1970s to about 36,000 in 1987.

Rocky Mountain offers over 350 miles of trails that lace the mountains, leading to every hidden valley and peak. Some of the more popular trails include Bear Lake Nature Trail (a half-mile loop around Bear Lake), Moraine Park Trail (a good introduction to local plants and animals), and Tundra Trail (offering a glimpse into the world above treeline).

While most hikers head for the popular scenic spots like Glacier Gorge and Longs Peak, fewer visitors see remote areas like the Mummy Range and Wild Basin. Of course, the well-traveled areas are justly popular—they include Rocky Mountain's most famous scenery.

Longs Peak, the park's most distinctive geographic feature, dominates Colorado's northern Rockies. To the Indians the peak along with neighboring Mount Meeker were "the Two Guides." French fur trappers called them *les Deux Oreilles,* "the Two Ears."

The first American reference to the peak was by Edwin James, a botanist on Major Stephen Long's "Expedition from Pittsburgh to the Rocky Mountains" in 1820. James noted in his diary that the mountains presented a "grand outline, imprinted in bold indentations upon the luminous margin of the sky." The first recorded ascent was in 1868 when a party led by Major John Wesley Powell reached the flat summit.

By the turn of the century Longs Peak was a popular tourist destination. Enos

► *A common hunter in Colorado's parklands, a Swainson's hawk perches atop a fence post.* STEWART M. GREEN

Mills, operating from his Longs Peak Inn, led groups to the summit. He climbed the mountain 297 times, including 32 ascents in August 1906. "Climbing a high peak occasionally," Mills later wrote, "will not only postpone death but will give continuous intensity to the joy of living."

Today about 7,000 climbers annually scale Longs Peak, most following the eight-mile-long Keyhole route. Rock climbers scale the peak's 1,700-foot east face, particularly 900-foot-high Diamond, the sheer upper half of the peak.

Long considered insurmountable, the Diamond was not ascended until 1960. Now rock climbers climb it by a variety of routes, usually taking one or two days. Other good climbs are the alpine faces of Chiefshead, Spearhead, Hallett Peak, and the Petit Grepon. Hundreds of other climbing routes crisscross the granite crags

on Lumpy Ridge north of Estes Park.

Park visitors enjoy the fishing. Rocky Mountain's streams and lakes harbor four species of trout: rainbow, brook, brown, and cutthroat. Fish live in 50 of the park's 156 lakes. Popular trout streams include Fall River, Big Thompson River, and the North Fork of the Colorado River.

The park service is reintroducing the greenback cutthroat trout, a threatened species native to Colorado, to its historical range on the east side of the park. Several lakes and streams are closed to fishing to help the repopulation effort. The fine for illegal possession of a greenback cutthroat trout is $5,000.

Many visitors come to see the park's mammals, with fifty-seven separate species ranging from shrews and mice to black bear and elk. Mule deer are common in Moraine Park and Beaver Meadows during mornings and evenings. The bighorn sheep herd, numbering almost 400, prefers to stay in the high elevations of the Mummy and Never Summer ranges but will occasionally drop down to use the natural mineral licks in Horseshoe Park. Moose thrive in the willow marshland in the Kawuneeche Valley. River otter, released in the Colorado River, are spreading across the divide to other rivers.

Around thirty black bears range through the park. No grizzly bears roam Rocky Mountain anymore, but it was once great grizzly country. In his book *The Grizzly, Our Greatest Wild Animal*, a classic study of animal behavior, Enos Mills wrote, "[the grizzly] is an animal of high type; and for strength, mentality, alertness, prowess, superiority, and sheer force of character he is the king of the wilderness. It is unfortunate that the Fates have conspired to end the reign of this royal monarch.

How dull will be the forest primeval without the grizzly bear! Much of the spell of the wilderness will be gone." The spell is broken—the park's last grizzly was sighted in the 1920s.

Between 3,000 and 4,000 elk live in the park, after being nearly extirpated at the turn of the century. "The elk are near the park's carrying capacity," says Kaye. "If we had a severe spring there would be a large elk die-off." A five-month hunting season on lands surrounding the park results in a yearly decrease of 500 animals. Bringing wolves back into the park is one option the park service is investigating to control the burgeoning elk population. The park, along with adjoining wilderness areas and national forests, includes 1,600 square miles of prime wolf habitat, enough for a pack of thirty wolves. However, says Kaye, "there will be a lot of dialogue with the public and with ranchers before we propose wolf reintroduction." The height of the elk mating season in late September and early October is the prime time to view Rocky Mountain's elk herd.

What is Rocky Mountain National Park—A wildlife refuge? An outdoor recreation park? A haven for wilderness ecosystems? It's all these and more. "Rocky Mountain has many other uses," says Kaye. "It's a watershed, a Class I airshed, and it's a resource for personal growth. People can not only learn what they can do outside, but they can see and understand how the world works and how they fit into it." Mills, who led the fight for the park's creation, had the same sentiments: "He who feels the spell of the wild, the rhythmic melody of falling water, the echoes among the crags, the bird songs, the wind in the pines...is in tune with the universe."

► *A Rocky Mountain iris, close cousin to the garden variety, blooms in Rocky Mountain National Park.* W. PERRY CONWAY

MUELLER STATE PARK

Mueller State Park lies in the morning shade of Pikes Peak. Covered with a canopy of coniferous forest, it rolls north and south along the western side of the peak. Rising here and there out of the canopy are rounded, granite domes and humped ridges. Below are rushing streams and valleys matted with willows.

The 12,094-acre park and wildlife preserve, a grand study in ecological diversity, not only harbors woodlands of pine, fir, and aspen but also protects crucial wildlife habitat from encroaching development. Lots of animals roam the park—deer, elk, black bears, bobcats, wild turkeys, eagles, and bighorn sheep.

Mueller is prime bighorn sheep territory, and it was the bighorns that led to the State of Colorado acquiring this parkland. While twenty-five bighorns live permanently in the park, the larger Pikes Peak herd migrates annually into the Fourmile Creek area for winter shelter and spring lambing. The property was crucial for their continued survival and health.

Colorado oilman W.E. Mueller, who quietly acquired a patchwork of former homesteads, state-school land, and cattle ranches over twenty-five years, had long permitted and encouraged the Colorado Division of Wildlife to conduct bighorn research on his ranch. Through this research, wildlife biologists learned how to control lungworm, a parasite that was destroying whole herds of bighorns.

By the early 1970s Mueller's ranch was one of the last lower-elevation bighorn ranges in Colorado. Growth around the

► *Dome Rock, a bulging granite peak, looms over hikers along Fourmile Creek in Mueller State Park. Mueller protects a wide swath of pristine woodlands, including valuable bighorn sheep habitat.* STEWART M. GREEN

ranch prompted the Colorado Division of Wildlife to begin negotiations with Mueller to buy and preserve this wildlife refuge. Negotiations stalled, but the Nature Conservancy, an environmental group, stepped in and purchased the Mueller Ranch in 1978 for $5.2 million. The Conservancy then resold the property to the State of Colorado.

Today, the Division of Parks and Outdoor Recreation manages the area as a state park, although the northern section is currently closed to public use. The southern area, dominated by 800-foot-high Dome Rock, is open for hiking, horseback riding, and fishing in Fourmile Creek. The parks division jointly manages this area with the Colorado Division of Wildlife to preserve the bighorn habitat.

Dome Rock, the heart of Mueller State Park, is a turreted granite skyscraper that looms over meandering Fourmile Creek. Other knobs, buttresses, and outcrops surround Dome Rock, dwarfed by its towering presence. The trail to the dome follows an old wagon road that parallels Fourmile Creek, making an eight-mile round trip from the parking area off Colorado Highway 67.

Mueller's history is as diverse as its natural beauty. Scattered around the park are over 100 historic sites. The collapsing cabin and corrals at the White brothers' 1890s ranch recall their horse stealing days. Both were hanged from nearby trees. There's an old mine that never produced an ounce of gold but provided its owner with a sizable income from dubious stock sales. All that remains of Jackrabbit Lodge is its chimney, but it was once a posh hunting camp complete with a baby grand piano and "ladies" from Denver.

Gentle terrain characterizes the closed northern part of the park. This rolling country seamed with shallow canyons and broken by ridges is in a development phase. Plans include a campground, picnic facilities, hiking trails, stables, and a visitor center. The area should be open by 1990.

Mueller is not only a sanctuary for wildlife and a rich blending of ecosystems but an enclave of wilderness on the doorstep of most of Colorado's population as well. Less than thirty miles from Colorado Springs and ninety from Denver, the park lies within two hours of over two million people. It's hardly a walled-in, off-the-beaten-track park, yet it remains a secret. Most passersby hurry down Highway 67, past the turnoff, and on to historic Cripple Creek.

If you do venture into the park, you'll find hidden places and see special things. After a day of wandering you'll undoubtedly agree with President Theodore Roosevelt's 1901 observation after passing through here, "Why, gracious me! Gentlemen, just look at that view! Isn't it marvelous? Wonderful! Wonderful!"

RIFLE FALLS STATE PARK

The canyon begins innocently enough. You drive north out of Rifle, turning onto Colorado Highway 325. The road skirts pastures and a golf course before easing through Rifle Gap, a spectacular break in the Grand Hogback. Turning northeast, you pass Rifle Gap Reservoir and spin into a narrow canyon with softly molded edges. After ten miles you reach Rifle Falls State Park. Unlike many natural wonders that signal their presence from afar, this park is tucked into an unimposing setting.

Rifle Creek rushes down the canyon past cliffs banded with tilting sandstone layers. A forest of pinyon pine and juniper wraps the hillsides, and groves of box elders cast dappled shadows over meadows on the valley floor. The creek bubbles over fallen logs and boulders. Upstream from this idyllic setting, a limestone cliff hangs across the valley. Shallow caves peer out from the cliff base.

Rifle Falls pours over the limestone curtain in three ninety-foot waterfalls. The water thunders off rocks below, filling the air with fine mist. State park rangers call this park "Colorado's Hawaii," and below the waterfall you see why. Ferns nestle in moist crevices, thick mats of spray-drenched grass and moss cover boulders below the falls, garter snakes and frogs hide in the wetness, and the smell of water perfumes the air. It looks as though an acre of Kauai's Na Pali Coast was airlifted from Hawaii and dropped in western Colorado. Water transforms the arid valley below Rifle Falls into an oasis, a blooming garden spot.

The falls themselves are unnatural. In the early 1920s, a small power plant diverted the stream's flow over the cliff. The resulting hydroelectric power fueled nearby Rifle until 1955 when the land was acquired by Colorado. The state park opened in the early 1970s.

Rifle Falls State Park is a pocket-sized park with only 220 acres at an elevation of 6,600 feet. Visitors come to view the spectacular falls, camp, and stroll on two miles of trail. Rifle Falls, with a visitation of only 25,000, remains a western slope hideaway, a place to find the unexpected—like a green Hawaiian valley.

► *Plunging off a limestone cliff, Rifle Falls cascades past a verdant garden. State park rangers call this idyllic parkland ''Colorado's Hawaii.''*
GEORGE WUERTHNER

GOLDEN GATE CANYON STATE PARK

From Panorama Point on the northern edge of Golden Gate Canyon State Park, the craggy spine of Colorado gleams in the evening light across the western horizon. The Indian Peaks stretch northward in a long row. Southwest lies Mount Evans, its snowy cirques hidden in shadow. As the sun sinks behind the mountains, clouds glisten gold, and the cliffs atop Tremont Peak, Golden Gate's high point, redden in the twilight.

Golden Gate, sixteen miles northwest of Golden, is a wilderness park typical of the Front Range above Denver. Consider its geography: knobby granite peaks reaching up to 10,400 feet, creeks whispering through pine and fir forests, meadows filled with grass and flowers and lined with quaking aspen, rough rock outcrops. Created in 1965, the park protects 8,787 acres of almost unspoiled wilderness.

Ponderosa pine, mountain mahogany, and serviceberry cover warm south-facing slopes. Thick stands of lodgepole pine, the ramrod straight tree used by Indians for tepee poles, cloak the park above 9,000 feet. Many wildflowers such as Indian paintbrush, aster, wild rose, columbine, and lupine carpet the mountain meadows. Golden Gate is a haven for animals, including mule deer, coyotes, porcupines, raccoons, and beavers.

Golden Gate is a hiking park. Almost sixty miles of trails weave and wend

► *From Panorama Point in Golden Gate Canyon State Park, the snow-covered Indian Peaks on the Continental Divide stretch across the western horizon.*
MARK HEIFNER/THE STOCK BROKER

► *Like Christmas ornaments,
raindrops decorate lupine leaves. A
member of the pea family, lupine is
common throughout Colorado.*
MICHAEL S. SAMPLE

among the mountains. One of the best is Mule Deer Trail. It leaves Aspen Meadow Campground, climbs past lodgepole pine and stunted aspen groves, and opens out at grassy Frazer Park. The meadow is full of sedges and reeds with splotches of summer color added by wild iris and buttercups. Campsites are tucked along Frazer's edge for backpackers. Turning west at Frazer Park, the trail meanders upwards to Promontory Ridge. A view of the Continental Divide unfolds beyond the ridge with afternoon thunderstorms crackling over the peaks.

Besides hiking, Golden Gate has other recreational uses. Fishermen like the shallow ponds along Ralston Creek on the park's southern perimeter, campers stay overnight, and day-trippers picnic in shady groves.

A few crumbling cabins scattered around Golden Gate are the only reminders of the park's history. In 1859 miner John Gregory abandoned his placer claim on Cherry Creek near today's Denver and traveled up Golden Gate Canyon to North Clear Creek six miles southwest of the park. On May 6 he started Colorado's first gold rush when he saw four dollars' worth of gold gleaming in his pan.

A flood of miners followed Gregory's route up Golden Gate Canyon through the future park and on to the goldfield at what was called Central City, "the richest square mile on earth." Gregory's trail became a toll road. Walkers paid fifty cents each and wagons $1.50. A.D. Richardson, a companion of Horace Greeley, described the road: "It seemed incredible that any animal less agile than a mountain goat could reach the summit, yet this road, only five weeks old, was beaten like a turnpike. Wagons carrying less than half a ton were drawn up by twenty oxen, while those descending dragged huge trees in full branch and leaf behind them as brakes." Two years later a better road was built up Clear Creek Canyon from Golden, and not a trace of the original road remains today.

Although miners roamed Golden Gate, they found no gold. Instead a few homesteaded the valleys, running cattle, farming potatoes, and cutting timber. The State of Colorado purchased 200 acres in 1960, and the park opened five years later.

Golden Gate, despite being close to Denver, remains unknown. "'How did I get here?' is the number one question asked at our Visitor Center," says one park ranger. A lot of folks, he went on, just "stumble on the park," unsure of which winding road actually brought them here. But when you do discover the park, you'll never forget it. Take a hike up to City Lights Ridge. The trail traverses a ponderosa pine forest, the trees smelling faintly like butterscotch. In the afternoon a wind comes up, shaking and rattling the tree branches. Bits and pieces of the Denver metro area, baking in the afternoon sun, waver above valleys dipping eastward. The world down there, the world of cities and men, seems far removed from this refuge of forest and grassland, of wind and storm.

CASTLEWOOD CANYON STATE PARK

Cherry Creek springs from the rolling country on the Palmer Divide separating the Platte and Arkansas watersheds between Denver and Colorado Springs. The creek gurgles north through grassland and past cattle ranches for fifteen miles before slicing into a coarse rock layer called Castle Rock conglomerate in ninety-foot-deep Castlewood Canyon. The conglomerate, deposited 25 million years ago by volcanic activity, forms cliffs that wall Cherry Creek in a narrow ten-mile-long canyon. Castlewood Canyon parallels Colorado Highway 83 about thirty miles south of Denver.

The 873-acre Castlewood Canyon State Park preserves the scenic gorge and a high plains environment. Located thirty miles east of the Rockies, it has more plants associated with the mountains than with the grasslands that surround the Palmer Divide. Receiving nineteen inches of annual rainfall, almost four more than Denver, the park harbors groves of ponderosa pine and Douglas fir on cool east- and north-facing canyon slopes. Quaking aspen flourish in moist draws, growing well below their normal 8,000-to-10,000-foot range. Grassy meadows, splotched with vetch and mustard, border the forests along the park road. Junipers and thickets of Gambel oak grow along the canyon rim.

This variety of plant communities makes Castlewood great wildlife habitat.

► *Showering visitors, Cherry Creek falls thirty feet off a lip of sandstone in the heart of Castlewood Canyon State Park. The waterfall formed after a burst dam farther upstream scoured the canyon floor on a stormy night in 1933.* BRUCE W. HILL

Prairie falcons, red-tailed hawks, and turkey vultures nest in the cliffs. Common birds include scrub jays, western bluebirds, magpies, rufous-sided towhees, turkeys, and canyon wrens. Skunk, rabbits, bobcats, coyotes, gray foxes, porcupines, Abert's squirrels, mule deer, and white-tailed deer populate the woodlands. Prairie rattlesnakes are frequently sighted in broken rock outcrops. Three fish species—longnose dace, fathead minnow, and black bullhead—inhabit shallow Cherry Creek.

Castlewood's human history centers around a dam built in the canyon in 1890. The lake was used for flood control, irrigation, and recreation. But leakage in 1891 led a panel of state engineers to examine the dam. They reported, "The dam has been built by irresponsible contractors under inadequate supervision." W.E. Alexander, the dam's owner, called the report "A low-lived attack from prejudiced persons" and claimed the idea of the dam breaking was "ridiculous."

The dam was built, however, on a natural spring which leaked into the foundation, and the ridiculous occurred on the night of August 3, 1933, when a heavy rainstorm burst the dam and sent a thirty-foot wall of water surging downstream to Denver. H.E. Paine, the dam's caretaker, warned authorities, and in a matter of hours 5,000 residents fled the creek's floodplain. The deluge reached Denver at 5:20 a.m., causing over $1 million in damages but claiming only two lives. The flood scoured Castlewood Canyon, excavating a deep channel and leaving barren walls. Cherry Creek now races through, roiling past chunks of fallen sandstone and shattering below a thirty-foot waterfall. The ruins of the dam still straddle the canyon.

Today, Castlewood is a gem of a park, one of those little-known, seldom-visited places; yet it's only a half hour's drive from Denver. Visitor uses are quiet—picnicking under the pines, hiking along Cherry Creek, and rock climbing. There are no established trails in the park, although two new trails are planned for the canyon rims. As a day-use area, the park allows no camping.

"Castlewood is a park still in the making," says Park Manager Susan Trumble. The master plan calls for a visitor center to be built on the canyon rim just off Colorado 83 to interpret Castlewood's geology and ecology. Until then it will remain a secret getaway of dense woodlands, rushing water, and rough crags.

BARR LAKE STATE PARK

The dusty trail passes under the low branches of cottonwood trees, then reaches across open fields filled with dry grass to more cottonwoods. Beside the trail, the quiet water of Barr Lake laps at a shoreline wreathed in downed branches and wavering smartweed. The silence of the afternoon breaks only with a magpie's raucous alarm and the periodic splashing of carp feeding in the warm shallows. A great blue heron, flying into the noon sun, arcs over the lake, its wings beating gently. To the west, beyond the lake, stretches the Front Range, with clouds building above snowcapped summits.

When you walk the lakeside trail in 2,610-acre Barr Lake State Park, twenty-five miles northeast of Denver, you see a typical riparian life zone. This ecosystem forms a boundary between the lake and the dry surrounding grasslands with cottonwoods, lush shrubbery, and marshes. The combination of water and plants attracts wildlife, including prairie dogs, cottontail rabbits, jackrabbits, pocket gophers, seven species of rats and mice, coyotes, red foxes, raccoons, skunks, and both mule and white-tailed deer. In fact, the southern part of Barr Lake is a wildlife refuge.

The park, a naturalist's paradise, also brings birders in flocks. "The great numbers of birds and the quality of the habitat make Barr Lake an exceptional resource," says Park Manager Carol Leasure. "Birdwatchers know it, too. We have people stop from all over the country." Over 300 of Colorado's 440 bird species have been identified here. A walk along the southern end of the 1,937-acre reservoir yields an assortment: a great blue heron, red-winged and yellow-headed blackbirds, a pair of cormorants, a flock of pelicans, a meadowlark on a fence post, western grebes, a western kingbird, and a soaring turkey vulture.

Barr Lake, formed by a dam built in 1907, was once a popular getaway for wealthy Denver socialites and sportsmen who used the lake for boating, hunting, and relaxation. But it hasn't always been a recreation area and wildlife refuge. Beginning in the 1930s, Denver transformed the lake into a sewage lagoon, and its smelly reputation still lingers with area residents. A 1965 flood flushed the lake, and Farmers Reservoir and Irrigation Company began restoring it. The Colorado Division of Parks and Outdoor Recreation acquired the area for its "unique environmental qualities" and opened the state park in 1977.

"Quite a few people describe Barr Lake as an island of habitat in a sea of development," Leasure explains, echoing a sentiment expressed by most park rangers along the Front Range. "It's not a question of if it's developed, but when." A new Stapleton Airport and Colorado Highway 470 are planned south of the park. The city of Brighton has annexed land on Barr Lake's western border. But, Leasure says, "we don't want to turn Barr Lake into a city park. It's not a playground or ball field. Our purpose is to make sure this good wildlife habitat is preserved."

Barr Lake's staff, along with the Colorado Division of Wildlife, operates a nature center with educational displays and programs. Over 4,000 Denver-area students come here each year to catch insects, chase butterflies, watch birds, and learn about the delicate web of life. "Parks have a prime opportunity to educate school kids about the natural world," Leasure says. In that education lies hope that Barr Lake's diverse and rich ecosystems will continue to flourish, that striped chorus frogs will sing in May, that sandhill cranes will rest on their southward autumn journey, that the wind will still ripple the prairie grass and stir the mirrored lake at dusk.

► *Common on shallow lakes, an eared grebe casts a watchful eye over a nest of eggs. Other nesting birds at Barr Lake include a spectacular rookery of great blue herons.*

SHERM SPOELSTRA

► *A blood-red sky dawns over Barr Lake State Park on the rolling prairie northeast of Denver. Cormorants perch atop bare cottonwoods along the lakeshore. Barr Lake is one of Colorado's best birdwatching areas, with over 300 species identified here.*

WENDY SHATTIL/ROBERT ROZINSKI

LORY STATE PARK

Lory State Park, twelve miles west of Fort Collins, bridges the transition from prairie to peak. East of the park, long sandstone hogbacks tilt upward before leveling into the Great Plains. West of the park tower the Rocky Mountains, their steep slopes broken with jagged crags.

Lory, a 2,419-acre park ranging in elevation from 5,430 feet on its eastern boundary to 7,015 feet above Arthur's Rock, was established as a state park in 1967 because it embraces three distinct life zones: the prairie grassland community, the mountain shrub community, and the ponderosa pine woodland. The grassland stretches along the valley between the hogback on the park's eastern border and the mountain rise. The mountain shrubland climbs steep south-facing slopes, thick with mountain mahogany, wild plum, and chokecherry and dotted with grassy meadows. The ponderosa pine woodland covers Lory's higher elevations.

Animals from both the mountains and the prairie live at Lory, including mule deer, coyote, fox, turkey, porcupine, Abert's squirrel, and prairie rattlesnake. Black bear, mountain lion, and bobcat are occasional visitors. Great horned owls nest in the hogback, while golden and bald eagles soar overhead. Over 100 butterfly species have been reported here.

About 75,000 visitors roam Lory annually, with 75 percent of them from adjacent Fort Collins, Loveland, and Greeley. "Lory State Park," says Park Manager Craig Bergman, "is one of the best-kept secrets in Colorado's state park

▶ *A pair of joggers cross an open grassland at Lory State Park. Visitors come for hiking, horseback riding, and nature study.* STEWART M. GREEN

system. People outside Larimer County just don't know about the park."

Hiking and horseback riding on thirty miles of trails are popular activities. Six backcountry campsites dot the ridge behind Arthur's Rock. Several paths thread through steep canyons to the knobby mountaintops above. The best trail climbs two miles up to the summit of Arthur's Rock. From the rock's summit (a rope is helpful for the last hundred feet) a spectacular panorama spreads out below. Forested slopes plunge down to

the hogbacks, their long ridges stretching south like frozen waves. Beyond lies a patchwork of farms and fields. Sunlight glints off distant reservoirs such as Boyd Lake, while water-skiers skim across nearby Horsetooth Reservoir. "On a clear day," Bergman says, "you can even see downtown Denver." Nearer at hand rise the snow-covered summits of Rocky Mountain National Park.

Other visitors picnic, sightsee, rock climb, or use the park to reach the western coves of Horsetooth Reservoir.

Controlled hunting is allowed in season. Most winters are mild enough to permit hiking, but cross-country skiers can slide along the trails after heavy snowfalls.

Lory State Park is well known as an equestrian center. The park annually hosts cross-country jumping competitions and 25- and 50-mile endurance rides. The Double Diamond Stables provides rental horses for those who don't own their own.

Lory State Park is an ecological island full of plants and animals from both prairie and peak. It's also an island for people. They hike its trails, soak up its sunshine and silence, and find inspiration and renewal in its daily rhythms and changing seasons.

COLORADO STATE FOREST STATE PARK

Colorado State Forest State Park is something of an enigma. It's not a park in the strict sense of the word, it's a state forest, a 72,000-acre preserve that under Colorado law has to make money. It does so through multiple uses: recreation, timber cutting, and cattle grazing. The money it generates contributes to Colorado's public school system.

The State Forest, Colorado's largest state park, was created in 1938. It stretches 30 miles down the western side of the Rawah Range between North Park, a large grassy basin, on the west and the Rawah Wilderness Area on the east. (Rawah means "wilderness" in Arapahoe.) Rocky Mountain National Park joins it on the south.

"The State Forest is simply breathtaking," says Monica Miller, state parks public affairs director. "If you were kidnapped in the middle of the night and woke up there you would swear you were in Switzerland."

Park elevations range from 8,400 feet on the western border to 12,951-foot Clark Peak in the Rawah Range. In

► *The Rawah Range, backbone of Colorado State Forest State Park, glows rosily above grassy North Park. The State Forest, Colorado's largest state parkland with 72,000 acres, is managed for multiple use. Income generated through timber sales, cattle grazing, and recreation benefits Colorado's public education system.*

STEWART M. GREEN

between lies a land of lofty tundra-covered peaks, U-shaped valleys (the result of glaciation 75,000 years ago), and remote lakes. Forests of lodgepole pine, spruce, fir, and aspen shroud the mountainsides. Dense stands of willows line streambanks, and sagebrush, rabbitbrush, and grass cover the lower elevations.

The State Forest's size and ecological variety make it prime wildlife habitat. Large mammals include bighorn sheep, deer, elk, black bear, and moose. "The State Forest is the best place in Colorado to see moose," says ranger Michael Hopper. The moose population, numbering thirty, usually keeps to the willow thickets along the Michigan River. The State Forest elk herd ranges between 600 and 800 animals. The park supports two bighorn sheep herds—the Rawah herd and the Never Summer herd—totaling about 125 sheep. Other wildlife include beaver, red fox, bobcat, coyote, mink, marten, marmot, and over 125 bird species.

The park also has excellent fisheries. "Kelly Lake is one of the only places in Colorado where you can fish for golden trout," notes Hopper. The state record for golden trout, an introduced California species, came from twenty-five-acre Kelly. The lake is accessible only by foot via a six-mile trail. Other lakes, including Ranger Lakes, Lake Agnes, and American Lakes, contain native cutthroat, rainbow, and brown trout. Brook trout inhabit the streams.

The State Forest is divided into several management zones, each with its own natural qualities and recreational opportunities. The most accessible zones are along Colorado 14 in the southern part of the park. The Middle Fork of the Michigan zone follows the highway corridor through the park, while the North Fork zone centers on the Michigan River watershed. Common pursuits, in addition to camping, are fly fishing, hiking, snowmobiling, and cross-country skiing.

The Crags Scenic Area looms above Colorado 14 with the jagged 13,400-foot Nokhu Crags dominating the view. Nokhu is an abbreviation of *Nea ha-no-Xhu*, meaning "eagle's nest" in Arapahoe. Mount Richtofen towers beyond the crags in Rocky Mountain National Park. The most popular hike in the State Forest climbs a half-mile trail to Lake Agnes, cradled in a timberline basin beneath the crags. To the east, another trail leads to American Lakes and Thunder Pass.

The Glacial Cirques Scenic Area lies below the Rawah crest in the park's midsection. Managed for backpacking and fishing and closed to motor vehicles, this zone encompasses wide valleys with meadows, spruce forests, tundra-covered mountain peaks, and high lakes. Over eleven miles of trails climb up to the lakes, including Kelly, Ruby Jewel, and Clear.

The northern zones are seldom visited. Access is limited by rough roads and adjoining private ranches. The Muddy Park and Medicine Bow Divide zones, managed as wilderness and range lands, form the upper half of the State Forest. "We just don't have the manpower to manage the north end," says Hopper.

One of the park's unusual features lies in the Muddy Park zone—the East Sand Dunes Natural Area. These active dunes sweep up against the Rawah Range. Most of the dunes are dormant, covered with grass, sagebrush, and trees. There is no access to the dunes other than by foot. Another dune field, the North Sand Dunes, lies outside the northern park boundary on BLM property.

Most people come to State Forest for camping and fishing, says Hopper. Of the 80,000 annual visitors, about 75 percent fish and camp. In addition to four campgrounds, the park offers primitive campsites and seven rental cabins.

Other activities include hiking and horseback riding on over fifty miles of maintained trails, mountain biking and four-wheeling on jeep roads, boating on North Michigan Reservoir, and hunting in season. Deer and elk are the most common quarry, but the state issues a few permits for moose, bighorn sheep, and bear.

Unlike many parklands, State Forest stays open for business all winter. The park maintains over fifty miles of groomed trails for snowmobilers and forty-five miles of ski trails for cross-country skiers. A concession rents yurts, large Mongolian platform tents, through the winter. "The skiers like them," says Hopper. "They're fancier than our cabins and you can set up a two- or three-day ski trip between them."

The Colorado State Forest is truly a land of many uses. It's a place to harvest timber and graze cattle. It's a place to camp, fish, hunt, hike, ski, bike, and boat. But it's also a wild place. The entire northern part of the park is true wilderness. "The biggest attraction of the State Forest," Hopper says, "is that it's not wall-to-wall people. If you go over the ridge to the Rawah Wilderness Area, it's usually crawling with people. But here, even though it's not designated wilderness, it's uncrowded." Monica Miller agrees, "The State Forest is totally unknown." ∎

People are individuals, and each finds his own park.

—George B. Hartzog, Jr., former director of the National Park Service

PARKS FOR PLAYING
RECREATIONAL PARKS

Colorado is hardly a land of lakes, rather it's a "mother of rivers," with four great rivers and a host of tributaries that flow from melting snow high atop the Continental Divide. The Colorado, Arkansas, North and South Platte rivers, and the Rio Grande have roots in Colorado, as well as the Dolores, Yampa, White, Gunnison, Cache La Poudre, Animas, and Purgatoire rivers.

But look at a map and you'll see that dams harness every river except the Yampa. The water, a precious commodity in a dry state, is stored and regulated for a wide range of uses. The state's rivers, particularly the Colorado, are the literal lifeblood for millions who depend on their perennial flow for household needs, electric power, food, and even clothing.

If you journey down any river in Colorado, from source to mouth, you see a revolution spawned by water technology. Deserts bloom with crops irrigated by Colorado water. Cities, developers, farmers, ranchers, oil-shale interests, miners, and power producers fight among themselves to garner more water for their needs. Meanwhile, environmentalists seek to leave minimum stream flows for wildlife and wilderness.

Besides industrial and agricultural uses, Colorado's impounded water serves another important need—recreation. The Colorado Division of Parks and Outdoor Recreation alone manages 28,000 acres of water for public use. These recreation parks range in size from Pearl Lake's 105 acres to Lake Pueblo's 4,000 acres. The National Park Service manages three reservoirs totaling 10,298 acres in Curecanti National Recreation Area.

Colorado's recreational parklands are these watery playgrounds. They're parks for people to enjoy, providing opportunities for camping, fishing, picnicking, boating, diving, swimming, waterskiing, windsurfing, and just about any other water sport you can imagine. While they're not established for scenic preservation, many like Curecanti National Recreation Area and Steamboat State Recreation Area offer spectacular scenery as an added bonus.

Pearl Lake S P
Steamboat Lake S R A
Boyd Lake S R A
Jackson Lake S R A
Barbour Ponds S R A
Bonny S R A
Rifle Gap S R A
Harvey Gap S R A
DENVER
Highline S R A
Sylvan Lake S R A
Island Acres S R A
Spinney Mountain S R A
Vega S R A
Paonia S R A
Eleven Mile S R A
Sweitzer Lake S R A
Crawford S R A
Curecanti N R A
Ridgway S R A
Lake Pueblo S R A
Lathrop S P
Mancos S R A
Navajo S R A
Trinidad S R A

► *Sunrise over peaceful waters at Boyd Lake.* STEWART M. GREEN

MOUNTAIN RECREATION AREAS

Great rivers are born on Colorado's mountain backbone—the Continental Divide. Rivers are here because mountains are here. If you stand atop the divide, snow, the raw material of rivers, whitens the valleys and peaks around you. Accumulating in thick blankets, snow supplies 75 percent of Colorado's water. Melting in spring, it cascades into alpine tarns, then gushes down through deep canyons to the Great Plains or the Colorado Plateau.

All across Colorado, dams still the swift rivers to form lakes. These artificial lakes meet Colorado's demand for water recreation. Almost anywhere you go in Colorado you'll find these lakes, but the best ones are Curecanti National Recreation Area, Eleven Mile, Steamboat Lake, Paonia, and Trinidad state recreation areas, and Pearl Lake State Park.

Curecanti National Recreation Area

It's open country where the Gunnison River squeezes past the town of Gunnison and rolls into a region of softly rounded hills. The river, however, flows only ten more miles before its currents slacken in Blue Mesa Lake. Below Blue Mesa Dam the Gunnison River drops into the deep abyss of the Black Canyon of the Gunnison and stills in Morrow Point Lake and again in Crystal Lake. This ladder of three lakes forms Curecanti National Recreation Area, a long, narrow parkland for fishing, boating, hiking, camping, and windsurfing on 10,298 acres of water and

▶ *Colorful aftermath of a summer storm, a rainbow arches over Blue Mesa Lake at Curecanti National Recreation Area. Fishermen, boaters, and boat-in campers recreate on this 9,000-acre lake, the largest lake wholly within Colorado.*
STEWART M. GREEN

30,228 acres of land. The Black Canyon of the Gunnison National Monument lies below Crystal Lake.

The three lakes are part of the Bureau of Reclamation's Upper Colorado River Storage Project. The dams harness the Gunnison River to store water and provide flood control and hydroelectric power. At the same time the lakes, managed by the National Park Service as Curecanti National Recreation Area, offer fun on their scenic waters and lengthy shoreline.

"We have a different type of visitor than other national park areas," says Curecanti ranger Dan Brown. "Our visitors know what they're coming here

for—boating and fishing." And the visitors, mostly Coloradans, do come—1,096,823 in 1987—making Curecanti Colorado's second-most-visited park after Rocky Mountain National Park. Other recreation includes windsurfing on the Bay of Chickens, hiking, birdwatching, hunting, and scuba diving.

Blue Mesa Lake, bordered by U.S. 50 west of Gunnison, is Colorado's largest lake. Stretching twenty miles from inlet to dam, it totals about 9,000 acres, depending on the lake level, and boasts ninety-six miles of shoreline. The lake forms three natural basins—Iola Basin on the east inlet side, Cebolla Basin in the middle, and Sapinero Basin on the west.

▶ *Denver & Rio Grande Engine 278 rests atop an original section of trestle, right, spanning Cimarron Creek in Curecanti. The railroad, operating from 1882 to 1949, climbed out of the Black Canyon at Cimarron. Another outdoor exhibit with corrals and stock cars details the railroad's importance to western Colorado.* RANDY TRINE

▶ *A castellated tower at Dillon Pinnacles, far right, overlooks Blue Mesa Lake. The coarse rock formed when surrounding volcanos spewed vast quantities of ash and boulders across the region over 30 million years ago. One of Curecanti's best trails climbs two miles up to the strangely carved pinnacles.*

STEWART M. GREEN

Blue Mesa Dam, an earthfill dam completed in 1965, towers 342 feet above the original river channel at the mouth of the Black Canyon. Blue Mesa is the park's most popular, most accessible, and most developed lake.

Flat-topped mesas surround Blue Mesa Lake, their rims capped with a layer of welded tuff spewed out by volcanos in the San Juan Mountains some 30 million years ago. Below the rims, erosion has carved strange rock forms in the breccia from volcanic activity in the West Elk Mountains, most noticeably at Dillon Pinnacles. Here a maze of grotesque towers, flying buttresses, gargoyles, balanced rocks, and fins provide an impressive backdrop to the blue lake. A two-mile-long trail follows the lake to a viewpoint below the pinnacles. Erosion left other spectacular spires above the West Elk and Soap Creek arms of the lake.

Blue Mesa Lake's deep waters (over 300 feet when full) attract fishermen who angle for kokanee salmon and brown, rainbow, Mackinaw, and brook trout. The cold water provides great habitat for Mackinaw, or lake trout, some weighing over thirty pounds. Rainbow trout are the lake's most common fish. During winter fishermen enjoy ice fishing for rainbow and brown trout. The Colorado Division of Wildlife, working with the U.S. Fish and Wildlife Service, stocks up to three million fish annually in Blue Mesa Lake.

In the upper Black Canyon, downstream

from Blue Mesa Dam, lies the secret heart of Curecanti. Here beneath the soaring walls of the canyon, Morrow Point and Crystal lakes lie remote and hidden. The only access to Morrow Point Lake from U.S. 50 is at Pine Creek just below Blue Mesa Dam. At the town of Cimarron on U.S. 50, a road winds one mile down to Morrow Point Dam to provide access to Crystal Lake.

Colorado Highway 92, turning north at Blue Mesa Dam, follows the precipitous north brink of the canyon, offering four developed scenic turnouts and three trails. There is no boat access from Highway 92. The scenery along here is spectacular, particularly at Pioneer Point and Hermit's Rest. The Black Canyon drops away dramatically, its dark, sweeping cliffs guarding the smooth lakes.

"Both Morrow Point and Crystal offer lots of solitude," says Ranger Dan Brown. "But they're both difficult to get onto." Boat access for Morrow Point Lake (eleven miles long with a twenty-four-mile shoreline and less than 300 feet wide through most of its length) is the one-mile-long Pine Creek Trail below Blue Mesa Dam. Boaters, limited to hand-carried craft, lug their gear down 232 steps to the lake.

"That trail is a real barrier for most visitors," says Brown. Those who make it onto the lake are usually fishermen, although the lake offers great canoeing, exploring, and primitive camping. For boatless visitors, Black Canyon Boat Tours gives daily intrepretive tours of the lake in the summer.

Another way to see the canyon is by foot. Curecanti Creek Trail, the park's best hike, follows the creek nearly 1,000 feet down two miles of trail from Pioneer Point on Colorado 92 to Morrow Point Lake.

Across the lake at the end of the trail is the area's most prominent landmark— Curecanti Needle. This 700-foot granite spike, chiseled away from the buttress behind, juts into the lake. The needle was world famous when it adorned the Denver & Rio Grande Railroad logo in the 1880s. Trains, steaming along the canyon railbed, stopped below the spire for admiring visitors.

The railroad climbed out of the Black Canyon at Cimarron, following today's road from U.S. 50 to Morrow Point Dam. Denver & Rio Grande Engine 278, perched atop an original section of trestle along the road, recalls the days when Cimarron was a "helper station" that added engines to trains climbing the 4 percent grade up over Cerro Summit. An exhibit at Curecanti's Cimarron Information Station details the railroad's importance in developing western Colorado and displays eight pieces of rolling stock, including an engine, tender, boxcar, caboose, sheep car, and cattle car. The railroad operated from 1882 to 1949.

Crystal Lake, accessible from Cimarron, is the least-visited lake in Curecanti. "There's a little rapid at the Crystal put-in below Morrow Point Dam," Brown says, "and every year a couple of overloaded boats flip there." Fluctuating water levels caused by frequent releases from Morrow Point Dam pose an additional boating hazard on Crystal. But those who do boat on the lake, six miles long with twenty miles of shoreline, find a landscape of rugged beauty, of granite walls, pine and fir forests, bighorn sheep, brown trout, and silence.

Most visitors don't realize that Curecanti harbors some of Colorado's most ancient archaeological sites. In 1984 the National Register of Historic Places listed seventy-nine prehistoric sites on 6,750 acres as the Curecanti Archaeological District.

One of the most exciting finds lies near Elk Creek. The park service intended to build a new headquarters on a flat hill overlooking Blue Mesa Lake, but archaeologists uncovered a number of sites hidden in the sagebrush—buried post holes and fire pits. The building site was moved a half mile west to its present location. Early paleohunters built crude shelters here up to 10,000 years ago. "There is a pattern of human use on the sites continuing until the last century when the Utes camped here," Brown says. "People even used the same firepits for thousands of years."

Eleven Mile State Recreation Area

The South Platte River begins on 14,286-foot Mount Lincoln above Hoosier Pass. After reaching South Park, a wide basin of rolling hills, the river unwinds like a great snake. At the valley corner opposite its birthplace, the South Platte abruptly exits South Park by cutting a channel through uplifted pink granite. Here a dam built in 1932 corrals its lively waters into 3,300-acre Eleven Mile Lake.

The Colorado Division of Parks and Outdoor Recreation manages the lake, an important part of Denver's water supply, and 3,900 acres of surrounding land as Eleven Mile State Recreation Area. Fifty

► *Morning mist shrouds fishermen along the south shore of Eleven Mile Lake, left.* STEWART M. GREEN

miles west of Colorado Springs, it is one of Colorado's most popular lakes.

Strong winds ruffle Eleven Mile in summer, churning waves against the lakeshore. Dotted with all types of boats from canoes to powerboats to sailboats, the lake is known not only for boating but also for great fishing. Trout, kokanee salmon (the state records for both angling and snagging salmon are here), and northern pike are regularly pulled from the lake. Ice fishing is Eleven Mile's most popular winter use.

Eleven Mile also offers hiking, boating, wildlife watching, waterfowl hunting, and camping. All water contact activities—swimming, wading, waterskiing, diving, and windsurfing—are prohibited.

Steamboat Lake State Recreation Area

Conical Hahns Peak dominates the view at Steamboat Lake State Recreation Area twenty-seven miles north of Steamboat Springs. Nestled in a grassy valley below the peak named after miner Joseph Hahn is 1,053-acre Steamboat Lake.

"Fishing and camping are our most popular activities," says Ranger J. Wenum. "The lake is real stable with little fluctuation in its level, so it makes an excellent trout fishery." Rainbow, cutthroat, brown, and brook trout inhabit Steamboat Lake. Other visitor uses include camping, hunting, waterskiing, swimming, windsurfing, and sailing. The park

► *A rainbow trout paddles through the shallow South Platte River above Eleven Mile State Recreation Area.*
RANDY TRINE

is a winter-sports mecca, with ice fishing, cross-country skiing, snow-mobiling, and sled-dog racing.

Steamboat's visitation totals 290,000 annually, and a survey of Colorado state park visitors identifies Steamboat as their favorite park. Dennis Scheiwe, the park's manager says, "all it takes is one visit and you're hooked."

Pearl Lake State Park

Pearl Lake State Park, Steamboat's sister park, sits five miles southeast of

Steamboat Lake. This park—105 acres of water and 169 acres of land—is a place for peace and quiet. All boats must observe wakeless speed, so it's a good canoeing lake. Trout fishing is by lure and fly only, and a forty-three site campground borders the lake.

Paonia State Recreation Area

Paonia State Recreation Area lies in the steep valley formed by Muddy Creek

► *Red-osier dogwood blossoms at Paonia State Recreation Area, above.* MICHAEL S. SAMPLE

► *Water-skiers cut across smooth water at Trinidad State Recreation Area, right. Formed by a 6,860-foot-long dam, the lake impounds the Purgatoire River.* STEWART M. GREEN

sixteen miles east of Paonia. The six-mile-long lake, bordered on the east by 12,094-foot Ragged Mountain, is like a Scandinavian fjord. Visitors stop by for fishing, waterskiing, boating, hunting, sightseeing, and camping.

Trinidad State Recreation Area

Trinidad State Recreation Area is hidden in southern Colorado three miles west of Trinidad. The park lies in the Purgatoire River Valley. The snowcapped Culebra Range, topped by 14,069-foot Culebra Peak, stretches west above the park, while angular 9,655-foot Fisher's Mesa dominates its southern skyline. Pinyon pine and juniper trees dot the surrounding low ridges and hillsides.

The park's 900-acre, three-mile-long lake was formed when the U.S. Army Corps of Engineers built a 6,860-foot-long dam for irrigation and flood control in the path of the Purgatoire River. The Purgatoire (its full name, *El Rio de las Animas Perdidas en Purgatorio,* means "the river of the lost souls in Purgatory")

is a river of history. Indians, their tepee rings visible at Carpios Ridge Picnic Area, often camped along the river. Dam construction revealed forty-eight archaeological sites within the park. Pioneers, following the Santa Fe Trail's Mountain Branch, crossed the river just below today's dam. Miners later dug coal from the black seams above the lake. Six mining communities—Jerryville, Piedmont, Saint Thomas, Sopris, Sopris Plaza, and Viola—sprang up along the river and are now submerged in the lake.

Almost 170,000 visitors come to the park annually. Fishermen catch rainbow

PRAIRIE RECREATION AREAS

Colorado's rolling plains spread over 40,000 square miles from Kansas to the Front Range. The land in between breaks with cottonwood-lined rivers—the Arkansas, South Platte, Republican, and Purgatoire; fields of sugar beets, wheat, and cantaloupes; ranches dotted with grazing cattle; and communities like Fort Morgan, Burlington, and La Junta. Out here, where the sky and horizon merge, where tawny brown stains the land, where the only sound is the rasping of the wind or your own breathing, out here an ocean of grass sweeps westward to a Rocky Mountain shore.

From out on the prairie, the Rocky Mountains are a mirage. Their peaks blend together in a ragged line breaking the horizon, and their snowy ridges gleam in the sun like alabaster towers. To pioneers crossing the plains in wagon caravans and on horseback, those distant peaks were like a dream. They were a cool oasis, a respite from the dust that parched the throat and the sun that beat down from a cloudless sky. The mountains still seem like a distant dreamland when you motor across the prairie, but now relief is close in six recreation areas—Lake Pueblo, Lathrop, Bonny, Jackson Lake, Barbour Ponds, and Boyd Lake—scattered across the plains.

Lake Pueblo State Recreation Area

The largest and most popular is Lake Pueblo State Recreation Area, with 15,755 acres of land, over 4,000 acres of water, and 1.5 million visitors a year—more than any other state parkland. Two-mile-long Pueblo Dam halts the Arkansas River to form the ten-mile-long reservoir, creating not only tap water for burgeoning cities like Colorado Springs, but a watery playground six miles from Pueblo's doorstep as well. Lake Pueblo's real purpose, as part of the Fryingpan-Arkansas water project, is to store water from west of the Continental Divide for cities on the drier Front Range.

Lake Pueblo is the most developed area in the state park system. "It's big, close to all of Colorado's major cities, has a year-round mild climate, and there's something there for everyone," says Monica Miller, state parks director of public affairs.

Fishermen, catching both largemouth and smallmouth bass, consider Lake Pueblo one of Colorado's premier bass fisheries. Like the best bass lakes, it has lots of shallow shoreline for spawning as well as deep water with nutrients promoting rapid bass growth. Other fish that inhabit the lake include rainbow trout, walleye, northern pike, and channel catfish.

Boating, waterskiing, and windsurfing are popular here. The lake's surface temperature averages 72 to 75 degrees in the summer. A swimming beach at the nine-acre Rock Canyon Swim Area below the dam fills up daily through the summer. Ten miles of paved bicycle trails link the park with the Pueblo trail system,

and brown trout, largemouth bass, channel catfish, walleye, crappie, and bluegill. Boaters, sailors, and water-skiers speckle the lake on busy weekends, while campers fill the campground.

Colorado's mountain recreation areas are places for people to pursue their outdoor interests. They're places where you can escape from the everyday world by adventuring down wilderness canyons, voyaging across mountain lakes, hiking through golden aspen groves, and discovering Colorado's history and prehistory. These are parks where you can get lost or, if you're lucky, find yourself.

► *A motorboat skims across Lake Pueblo. Beyond rises Pikes Peak, a sharp contrast to the desert scrubland surrounding the lake.*
STEWART M. GREEN

hooks in for rainbow trout, channel catfish, crappie, bass, and perch. Lathrop, designated a state park in 1962, has two campgrounds, picnic facilities, and a nine-hole golf course leased to Walsenburg. The western part of the park, a wildlife management area, opens for waterfowl hunting in season.

A scenic trail, looping north from Martin Lake for two miles, passes a maze of buff-colored boulders and climbs onto a ridge. Along the ridge you can see Pikes Peak almost 100 miles north. To the west lies a half circle of mountains—Greenhorn Mountain, Mount Maestas, the long rib of the Culebra Range, and the Spanish Peaks. To the east sweeps the shortgrass prairie, unbroken except by a distant horizon.

Bonny State Recreation Area

Bonny State Recreation Area, twenty-five miles north of Interstate 70 and Burlington in eastern Colorado, almost belongs to Kansas. The land tilts slowly into the broad valley of the Republican River. Blocking the river a few miles before it escapes into Kansas, a dam the U.S. Bureau of Reclamation built for flood control in 1951 stretches across the valley. Today the state of Colorado manages the lake as Bonny State Recreation Area.

The visitor brochure calls Bonny "a recreational oasis." Visitors from Colorado, Kansas, and Nebraska flock to 1,900-acre Bonny Reservoir to lie on its sparkling beaches, camp in its four campgrounds, waterski and swim in its warm water, or just kick off their shoes

while horseback riders follow Boggs Flat Horse Trail across a dry mesa south of the lake. Campsites and picnic areas complete the facilities.

Hikers can use several maintained trails. The Rock Creek Canyon Trail meanders among cottonwoods along the Arkansas River below the dam. Arkansas Point Trail leads to a rocky bluff overlooking the lake. After the viewpoint the trail follows the southeastern arm of the lake, winding through dry canyons and traversing yucca-covered slopes. Mule deer browse on sagebrush along the arroyos, and the songs of meadowlarks echo off sandstone cliffs. Out along the lakeshore you can cast your line, sit back on a warm boulder, soak up the sun and silence, and forget about the rest of the world.

Lathrop State Park

Lathrop State Park lies on the northern edge of a wide valley three miles west of Walsenburg off U.S. 160. The Spanish Peaks, called *Huajatolla* or "Breasts of the World" by the Pueblo Indians, rise like hazy apparitions from the windy, undulating foothills on the western horizon.

Lathrop has two reservoirs—Martin and Horseshoe lakes, with 320 acres of water between them. The park's 1,050 acres of land are rolling countryside, bordered on the north by a scrubby volcanic hogback. Most visitors head straight to the lakes for boating, canoeing, swimming, and fishing. Anglers toss their

► *The Culebra Range dominates the view at Lathrop State Park. The park's two lakes attract fishermen and boaters.*
WENDY SHATTIL/ROBERT ROZINSKI

and wade into this rippling prairie sea. Bonny is one of Colorado's prime warm-water fisheries, with a thriving population of walleye, northern pike, freshwater drum, white bass, largemouth and smallmouth bass, crappie, bluegill, bullhead, and channel catfish.

Bonny is also recognized as one of Colorado's premier birdwatching areas. Its location on the Central Flyway, the main north-south thoroughfare for wintering birds, brings up to 70,000 birds of 250 species during spring and fall migrations. In winter up to 50,000 birds call Bonny home, including snow and Canada geese, ducks, and golden and bald eagles. Besides bringing birdwatchers, the vast flocks of birds bring waterfowl hunters in autumn.

One of Bonny's most interesting aspects is also its least known. Scattered across the park are four small areas, totaling eighty acres, that form the Bonny Prairie Natural Area. Designated by the Colorado Department of Natural Resources as an endangered plant community, these lands preserve a remnant of the once vast little bluestem loess grassland. Ecologists note less than thirty North American locations of this grassland that once covered much of the western Great Plains. This rare grassland makes Bonny more than just another lake; it's also a reservoir of biologic diversity.

Jackson Lake State Recreation Area

Jackson Lake State Recreation Area, a 1,910-acre reservoir built in 1902 for irrigation, provides recreation for almost 300,000 visitors annually. The cotton-

► *Fun in the sun: a mother and children relax on a lakeshore, right. Prairie parklands offer warm summer water for swimming and wading.*
MICHAEL S. SAMPLE

► *Hikers explore a typical prairie marsh at Barbour Ponds State Recreation Area, far right, alongside Interstate 25 north of Denver. Fishermen pursue warm-water species, including bluegill, bass, and channel catfish in the park's four ponds.*
STEWART M. GREEN

wood-lined lake, eighty miles northeast of Denver off Interstate 76, draws lots of Denver folks for water sports, warm-water fishing, camping in 200 sites, building sand castles on the beaches, hiking along the north shore, and birdwatching along the lake and nearby South Platte River. Winter activities include hunting, skating, ice fishing, observing bald eagles, and cross-country skiing.

Barbour Ponds and Boyd Lake State Recreation Areas

Barbour Ponds and Boyd Lake state recreation areas both border Interstate 25; Barbour is thirty miles north of Denver and Boyd Lake is sixty-five. Each has a distinctive personality. Barbour Ponds is a pocket-sized park, with only sixty acres of land and eighty acres of water filling four ponds on the south bank of the St. Vrain River. Being adjacent to I-25, Barbour lends itself to convenient recreation. "The park is very popular for family outings," says Ranger Jeff Riddle. Since the area's opening in 1972, visitors have camped, fished for bluegill, bass, channel catfish, and crappie, canoed on the calm ponds, and hiked the boardwalk trail through the lakeside marsh. All this is tucked into a little refuge alongside a busy interstate highway.

Boyd Lake, like the other prairie reservoirs, is a water sports paradise. The park, adjoining Loveland and Interstate 25, lies within an hour's drive of the majority of Colorado's population. Boyd Lake is more lake than land, with 1,747 acres of water compared to the 197 acres of parkland on the lake's western edge. Well known for its water recreation, Boyd hosts annual sailboat regattas and hydroplane powerboat races. Other activities include camping, warm-water fishing, and swimming.

Eastern Colorado is often considered a poor stepchild to the state's majestic mountain province. It's a land that is both harsh and beautiful. It's a dry grassland where the wind never seems to stop blowing. Yet at the same time over 80 percent of all Coloradans call it home, and it holds the state's most productive farmland. When you venture onto the prairie, you discover a rich history left by mountain men, immigrants, and explorers; you see a land full of animal and bird life; and you find six state recreation areas that offer the best of Colorado's high plains.

PLATEAU RECREATION AREAS

The western plateau country makes up one-fifth of Colorado. It begins where the mountains dip down in spectacular fashion, their forested slopes giving way to red-rock mesas and valleys. The deeply sculptured plateau, a region of horizontal sedimentary rocks, is high (generally over 5,000 feet), dry (less than ten inches of annual rainfall), and lonesome (most of the population lives in Grand Junction, Montrose, and Cortez). It's a region of dusty rivers, sharply incised canyons, flat mesas, and hot days. Come summer, when the daily highs creep into the upper nineties, most western Coloradans head for the cool water in Navajo, Highline, Island Acres, Crawford, Sweitzer Lake, Rifle Gap, Vega, Ridgway, and Mancos state recreation areas.

Navajo State Recreation Area

Forty-five miles southeast of Durango is the principal reservoir for the Navajo Indian Irrigation Project. This 15,600-acre lake (3,000 acres in Colorado) straddles the Colorado-New Mexico border. Fed by the Piedra and San Juan rivers, the water is diverted south to the Navajo reservation to make their desert lands green with crops.

Before the lake was filled, archaeologists uncovered 1,500-year-old underground dwellings built by the Anasazi Indians. Padres Escalante and Dominguez passed through on their 1776 expedition to find a route from Santa Fe to California. Later, the Denver & Rio

Grande Railroad pushed narrow-gauge tracks through the park. The abandoned railbed still remains for hikers to trace.

Most of Navajo Lake lies in New Mexico, but Park Manager Larry Haines says, "we have a lot of people come to our end because it's less crowded." Navajo averages about 120,000 visitors a year on the Colorado side.

Steady winds make Navajo ideal for sailing and windsurfing. Its size makes it great for waterskiing. Houseboats are also common. Haines says, "People put their houseboats in and we won't see them for a week. People like cruising the lake; there are lots of interesting canyons and

coves to explore. It's a scaled-down version of Lake Powell."

Anglers reel in bluegill, catfish, crappie, largemouth bass, rainbow trout, northern pike, and kokanee salmon. In addition to a large campground, Navajo boasts Colorado's largest boat ramp—eighty feet wide and a quarter-mile long—and an airstrip for fly-in visitors.

Highline State Recreation Area

Highline State Recreation Area, fifteen

► *Testing his luck on a summer evening, an angler casts into a secluded arm of Highline Lake. Among the park's twenty-five fish species are bass, crappie, trout, northern pike, and channel catfish.* STEWART M. GREEN

► *Picnickers, left, under a cottonwood canopy enjoy a manicured lawn at Highline State Recreation Area. Visitors flock to the park, sixteen miles west of Grand Junction, for water sports in the hot summer months.* STEWART M. GREEN

► *Summer waders cool off in one of Island Acre's two ponds, right. The park preserves a small slice of the Colorado River's floodplain in De Beque Canyon.*
MICHAEL S. SAMPLE

miles west of Grand Junction, lies at the western end of the wide Grand Valley. The state park brochure calls Highline, with its mowed lawns, shady cottonwoods, picnic tables, and campsites, "a city-like park in a rural setting." While only six miles north of Interstate 70, no highway signs lead the casual passerby to the park, leaving Highline to residents who have discovered its simple charm.

Highline is a verdant oasis developed for water-based recreation on its two reservoirs—160-acre Highline Lake and fourteen-acre Mack Mesa Lake. Highline Lake, the only multiple-use lake close to Grand Junction, is popular for speed-boating, waterskiing, and swimming. The wakeless northern part of the lake attracts fishermen and migratory waterfowl. Birdwatchers have identified over 150 species here, including great blue heron, white pelican, snowy egret, Canada geese, killdeer, pheasant, and meadowlark.

Mack Mesa Lake, northwest of Highline Lake, harbors many birds that nest among the cattails lining the lakeshore. Yellow-headed blackbirds perch among tamarisk; killdeer cry from bunchgrass; and flotillas of geese drift across the lake. Mack Mesa is a popular trout lake, particularly in spring and fall. "I just love this little lake," says retired Grand Valley farmer Dick Greene. "Why? Because you can sit here and watch the world go by."

Island Acres State Recreation Area

Fifteen miles east of Grand Junction on the Colorado River is another recreational jewel—Island Acres State Recreation Area.

Colorado's smallest state park, a mere 139 acres, lies along the Colorado River as it pours through De Beque Canyon. The river runs fast through the 800-foot-deep gorge past stair-stepped sandstone slopes and spills over small rapids and flood control dams. "Island Acres," says Park Manager Richard Fletcher, "is the only state park that preserves part of the Colorado River ecosystem." Thickets of tamarisk mark the riparian zone along the river. Managed as a wildlife area, this zone supports ducks, muskrat, beaver, and great blue heron.

Island Acres, hemmed in by the river on the west and Interstate 70 on the east, was originally Island Ranch, an island planted with peach trees. But a levee built in the 1950s swung the river to its present course, and the old channel, filled with sand, was converted to hay production and grazing. In 1966 the Colorado

Department of Highways purchased the property and extracted gravel from it for the construction of I-70. The resulting gravel pit created two lakes that the state transformed in 1967 into a riverside park.

Being adjacent to I-70, it's not surprising that Island Acres is used by out-of-staters for rest and relaxation. While the park has a campground, most users are day visitors. A popular pursuit is trout fishing; a concrete pier allows handicapped fishing access. The park's open space is irrigated with river water, keeping Island Acres green, cool, and inviting during the summer.

Crawford State Recreation Area

Crawford State Recreation Area, one mile south of Crawford, nestles in the shadow of the 194,000-acre West Elk Wilderness Area. Sharp peaks crowd the park's eastern horizon, including 800-foot-high Needle Rock, a volcanic neck intruded into sedimentary layers as molten rock some 28 million years ago. Black Canyon of the Gunnison National Monument lies fourteen miles south of Crawford.

The Colorado State Parks map calls Crawford "THE place for a true escape." It is, indeed, peaceful and remote. Visitors use the park's 400-acre reservoir for fishing, boating, and water sports. Campers stay in one of three campgrounds. Waterfowl flock to the lake. Great blue herons probe the lake's shallows, killdeer poke along the shoreline, and Canada geese claim the south marsh.

Sweitzer Lake State Recreation Area

Sweitzer Lake State Recreation Area, a 137-acre lake three miles south of Delta off U.S. 50, is a park for traditional water recreation. Fishermen are advised, however, not to eat the fish due to high concentrations of selenium that occur naturally in the Mancos shale underlying the lake. The park is an ideal afternoon stop, a perfect place to picnic on shady grass and watch the kids go wading.

▶ *A setting moon rims the horizon above campers at Crawford State Recreation Area, above.* STEWART M. GREEN

► *In a spray of white water, hotdog water-skier Albert Romero, left, skims over Sweitzer Lake.*
GEORGE WUERTHNER

Rifle Gap State Recreation Area

The Grand Hogback is one of Colorado's most distinctive geographic features. If you look at a satellite map of the state, you can trace its S-shape from Meeker to Glenwood Springs. It marks the geographic boundary between the Rocky Mountains and the Colorado Plateau. Eight miles north of Rifle, Rifle Creek slices through a deep notch in the Hogback, forming a natural break called Rifle Gap. A dam plugs the gap here, creating a reservoir administered as Rifle Gap State Recreation Area.

The 350-acre reservoir, surrounded by 1,484 acres of land, attracts 100,000 people annually. Fishermen cast for rainbow and brown trout, walleye, and smallmouth and largemouth bass. Hunters use the park in autumn as a base camp for venturing into the surrounding White River National Forest. Campers stay in one of four campgrounds. The park also hosts the usual water sports like swimming, waterskiing, sailing, and windsurfing, as well as the unusual like scuba diving.

Vega State Recreation Area

Vega State Recreation Area lies sixty-two miles east of Grand Junction off Colorado 330 on the northern flank of Grand Mesa. One of western Colorado's principal features, Grand Mesa juts west from the Continental Divide with elevations between 10,000 and 11,000 feet. The fifty-square-mile plateau, capped by ancient lava flows, receives over thirty inches of annual precipitation, mostly snow. Dense forests of aspen, spruce, and fir sweep down to Vega at 8,000 feet, covering the mesa's slopes. A shallow valley, circled by forested peaks and carpeted with wildflowers, cradles the 900-acre reservoir.

The lake forms a playground for boaters, fishermen, water-skiers, and other recreationists. Vega attracts almost 100,000 visitors every year. Vega is recognized as a superb trout fishery, regularly yielding rainbow trout up to five pounds.

Ridgway State Recreation Area

Lofty mountains surround Ridgway State Recreation Area, twenty-five miles south of Montrose on heavily traveled U.S. 550. The craggy summit of Mount Sneffels and a long ridge of alpine peaks rise in the south. On the east towers Chimney Peak and blocky Courthouse Mountain. Mike Leak, state parks landscape architect, says, "The views in this area are second to none."

State parks Public Affairs Director Monica Miller promises that Ridgway, scheduled to open in 1989, "will be western Colorado's premier water-sports area." The park will have a seven-lane boat ramp, marina, 275 campsites, hiking trails, picnic areas, and a visitor center. Biologists studying the lake, however, say it probably will not be a good fishery due to the Uncompahgre River's high mineral

► *Catch of the day: a proud fisherman displays trout pulled from Vega Lake. Anglers regularly catch five-pound trout at Vega.*
GEORGE WUERTHNER

content. A dam spanning the river will create the 1,030-acre reservoir.

Mancos State Recreation Area

The newest recreation park is Mancos State Recreation Area, thirteen miles northeast of Mesa Verde. One of the prettiest recreation areas, Mancos offers dramatic views of the La Plata Range, the westernmost extension of the Rocky Mountains in Colorado. Recreation at Mancos centers around Jackson Gulch Reservoir, a 215-acre lake. The park has a campground, picnic areas, and a boat ramp.

When you wander through Colorado's plateau country—through canyons lined with sandstone, across valleys filled with grazing cattle, and around mesas etched against the indigo sky—you'll find hidden places that offer water and warmth: Colorado's eight plateau recreation areas. Each with its own personality, will bring you back again and again to this land of far horizons. ■

No nation has ever fallen through having too many parks.

—ENOS MILLS

PARKS FOR PEOPLE URBAN PARKS

On a rocky ridge pines sway in the wind; high above a hawk circles. The Great Plains stretch east to a flat horizon, while to the west lie the jagged peaks of the Continental Divide. Up on the ridge the only sound is the moan of the wind. Wilderness? No. It's one of Colorado's urban parks. Houses, subdivisions, malls, and highways hug the mountain slopes 3,000 feet below, but on the rocky heights is a world of silence and beauty.

Denver owns one of the nation's largest city park systems, and both the City of Boulder and Jefferson County taxed themselves to acquire new parklands for their growing populations.

The Colorado Division of Parks and Outdoor Recreation, with nine state parks within an hour's drive of the Denver metro area, runs two of them—Cherry Creek and Chatfield state recreation areas—especially for Denver residents, providing a range of activities from birding to powerboating.

The counties that surround Denver, including Douglas, Arapahoe, and Adams, are beginning to address their residents' needs for more parks. Other counties and cities, including Larimar County, El Paso County, and Colorado Springs, continue to develop park systems full of both spectacular natural areas and places for active recreation.

Every Colorado city, town, and community owns public parkland from small grassy squares in towns like Saguache and Placerville to huge sections like Boulder County's 32,000 acres. Our urban parks preserve places close to our homes, some possess great scenery, some provide a variety of recreation, some offer sports. These are parks that help us understand our history, teach us about nature, and give hours of enjoyment. These are parks for people.

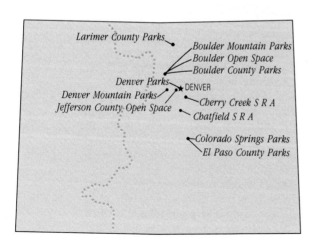

DENVER PARKS

A group of Georgia prospectors set up camp at the confluence of the South Platte River and Cherry Creek in 1858. The following year hordes of hopeful gold-fevered emigrants arrived at the settlement, called Denver City after James Denver, governor of the Kansas Territory. Most stopped only to rest before trekking into the Central City goldfield, but a few stayed behind, setting up shops, saloons, churches, banks, and hotels. By 1860 Denver had a population of 4,749. From these humble beginnings Denver grew to a metropolitan area encompassing six counties, 5,000 square miles, and almost 1.5 million people.

As early as 1872 Denver Mayor Joseph Bates suggested acquiring parkland. In 1875 William Byers, editor of the *Rocky Mountain News,* warned that Denver would not be a perfect city until "a public park is provided like Central Park on Manhattan Island." An 1878 bill introduced in the Colorado legislature allowed Denver to purchase 1,280 acres of state land divided into two 640-acre parcels. These two parks, Sloan Lake on the west and City Park on the east, began Denver's long love affair with its parklands.

Today, Denver's park system has 4,000 acres within Denver, almost 14,000 acres of mountain parks, fifty-seven miles of off-street trails, thirty miles of parkways, and thirty recreation centers. The parks department also manages sports and cultural facilities, including the Denver Zoo, Botanic Gardens, and Mile High

► *Ferns thrive in the moist shade of a granite boulder, left.* STEWART M. GREEN

► *"Every park is a place of refuge, a place wherein wildlife thrives and multiplies," wrote Enos Mills. At Washington Park, one of Denver's nine large urban parks, a girl feeds ducks along the lakeshore.* GEORGE WUERTHNER

Stadium, home of the Denver Broncos.

Within Denver's city limits lie nine large parks, each more than eighty acres, that provide green space for residents. Four of the parks—City Park, Washington Park, Cheesman Park, and Berkeley Lake—have been nominated for historical designation. These four are landscaped places of meadows, lakes, fountains, trees, and views.

City Park, east of downtown Denver, is the most famous of the urban parks. In 1881 Denver park commissioner Richard Sopris began developing the 640-acre parcel. Over the next thirty years the sagebrush-covered prairie was transformed with hundreds of trees, formal gardens, lakes, statues, and a zoo. Now City Park breaks the cityscape with mature forests of spruce, fir, maple, elm, oak, and cottonwood; colorful flower beds; grand views of the burgeoning skyline and the mountains; a modern zoo and the Denver Museum of Natural History; and a golf course, foot and bike paths, and picnic grounds. City Park maintains its original intent: to preserve within the city a sense of nature.

Beyond the city lies Denver's other skyline—the Rocky Mountains. The 13,755-acre Mountain Park System is the largest landholding of the Denver Parks and Recreation Department. Much of the land remains undeveloped, functioning as

► *City Park, far left, modeled after New York's Central Park, offers mature shade trees, multihued flower beds, lakes, and playing fields to bicyclists, joggers, picnickers, and fun-seekers.*
JAMES FRANK

► *With 10,000 seats, Red Rocks Amphitheater, left, attracts Denver concertgoers to Red Rocks Park. One nineteenth-century writer said, "If the Red Rocks had been located in Egypt or in Greece, the park would have been included among the ancient Wonders of the World." The 300-million-year-old rocks were first described by the Hayden Survey in 1869.* STEWART M. GREEN

items such as the saddle, guns, and costumes he used in his Wild West show. Cody died in Denver in 1917.

Other parks spread out across the mountain backdrop. Genesee Park, the largest in the system at 2,400 acres, straddles Interstate 70 above Denver. Buffalo and elk graze in pens along the highway. Genesee offers three picnic areas and spectacular views of the Continental Divide to the west. Several well-used parks—Bergen, Cub Creek, Corwina, and O'Fallon—surround Evergreen. They're all popular getaways for picnicking and hiking.

Denver's alpine Echo Lake and Summit Lake parks lie in the shadow of 14,264-foot Mount Evans. Echo Lake is a popular hiking and fishing park, while Summit Lake, nestled in a glacial cirque on Mount Evans' north flank, has rare alpine flowers and wildlife. Nearby is the

as open space and wildlife preserves. But 8,505 acres are open for public use, providing recreation such as picnicking, camping, fishing, and hiking. A few mountain park units are developed, including Winter Park Ski Area, Buffalo Bill Museum, and the famed 10,000-seat

amphitheater in Red Rocks Park.

The Buffalo Bill Memorial Museum and Grave commands the summit of Lookout Mountain above Golden. The museum exhibits memorabilia from the life and times of William F. Cody, otherwise known as Buffalo Bill. On display are

Mount Goliath Alpine Unit, a botanical park located on a rounded spur of Mount Evans. The M. Walter Pesman Trail leads through bristlecone pines at timberline to the alpine tundra zone.

In addition to urban and mountain parks, Denver's park system includes open-space corridors flanking the South Platte River and its tributaries. The Platte River Greenway follows the river's course through Denver. In 1974 the nonprofit Platte River Greenway Foundation and Denver Parks and Recreation began restoring the much-abused South Platte River within Denver. The results are apparent today. Hikers, joggers, and bicyclists follow an 11.5-mile concrete trail, while kayakers shoot manmade rapids in sight of Denver's skyline. The river has also reemerged as a wildlife area with the return of beaver, muskrat, ducks, and geese. Pocket parks and hundreds of open-space acres dot the Greenway.

Denver was fortunate to have farsighted civic leaders who acquired and developed parklands for future generations. The seed they planted has grown and matured, and now the challenge of the future is clear. With its growing population, Denver needs more parks. The city, land-locked by surrounding municipalities, is 84 percent developed. Little open space remains within the city limits for parkland. While Denver's existing parks ensure a system for the future, the city needs to acquire and manage new parks outside the city limits in conjunction with neighboring communities. As Denver park planner S.R. DeBoer noted in 1929, "Though beauty may be destroyed very easily, it hardly ever slips into a plan without someone's effort."

► *Horseback riders trot through grassy fields in 3,002-acre White Ranch Park, the largest parkland in Jefferson County's open-space system. Almost twenty miles of trails thread through the park's forests and grasslands.*
STEWART M. GREEN

JEFFERSON COUNTY OPEN SPACE

Prairies, foothills, canyons, and mountains define 780-square-mile Jefferson County. Jeffco, as locals call it, encompasses the western half of the Denver metro area and includes Lakewood, Colorado's fourth-largest city with 125,000 residents, along with Arvada, Wheat Ridge, and Golden. Over the last twenty years these communities have grown rapidly, spreading subdivisions, shopping malls, and highways across the county. But when you look at a map of Jefferson County,

you see that its citizens planned well, leaving large blocks of land undeveloped for parks and open space.

Since 1972 when Jefferson County residents established an open-space program by levying a county-wide .5 percent retail sales tax, the county has acquired 16,000 acres. Anthony Sabatini, chairman of the Open Space Advisory Committee, calls Jefferson County's program "one of the finest models in the nation."

This superb collection of parklands

attracts over a million visitors a year. A trail system allows hikers, backpackers, cross-country skiers, and horseback riders to penetrate the mountain parks, while urban trails offer recreation for walkers, bicyclers, and joggers.

White Ranch Park, the largest unit at 3,002 acres, was a working cattle ranch from 1913 to 1969. Straddling the mountains north of Golden, its wide meadows and ponderosa pine woodlands invite hikers to explore almost eighteen miles of trails leading to backcountry campsites and spectacular views of Denver. A display at the parking area illustrates how the meadows were hayed with horse-drawn farm implements. Animals, including mule deer, bear, mountain lion, and turkey, populate the southern part of the park, which is managed as a wildlife preserve.

Mount Falcon Park, 1,408 acres atop the mountains west of Morrison, was once the estate of John Brisben Walker, a wealthy land speculator and owner of the Stanley Steamer Company. Walker was a man with two visions: to build a summer White House for presidents and to preserve Colorado's spectacular lands as public parks. Success eluded him on his first dream. Construction never went beyond the laying of a foundation and marble cornerstone on a ridge overlooking Red Rocks Park, even though thousands of school children each donated ten cents toward the project.

His second dream was more successful. Today Walker's estate and the ruins of his burned mansion (built in the early 1900s) are open to the public. Trails, attracting hikers and equestrians, wend through forests and meadows, stopping at scenic views and picnic shelters. The view from the Summer White House ruins is marvelous: the corrugated sandstone slabs of Red Rocks Park sweep up against Mount Morrison across the valley, and the distant spires of downtown Denver pierce the horizon.

Other Jefferson County parklands include Means Meadows west of Evergreen, Matthews-Winters Park on either side of I-70 south of Golden, Green Mountain Park, a foothills park west of Lakewood, and the Hiwan Homestead Park in Evergreen, which preserves a seventeen-room log home built in the 1880s. Placed on the National Register of Historic Places in 1974, Hiwan has a living history program to preserve the county's rich heritage.

CHERRY CREEK AND CHATFIELD STATE RECREATION AREAS

Every city needs to provide a variety of recreational opportunities for its residents. Denver, in addition to its mountain and urban parks, has two watery playgrounds on its south side—Cherry Creek and Chatfield state recreation areas, lying, respectively, southeast and southwest of the city. Both are reservoirs formed by flood-control dams.

Cherry Creek State Recreation Area opened in 1959 as the first state park. "We have over thirty different activities here," says park ranger Ron Dunlap. But, according to Dunlap, most visitors come to fish. "Cherry Creek is the number-one fishery in Colorado for the number of fish stocked and fish caught. They fish the heck out of this lake in the summertime." The 880-acre lake holds trout, pike, catfish, wiper, bass, and walleye. The state record walleye, sixteen pounds, eight ounces, and thirty-four inches long, was pulled from Cherry Creek Reservoir.

Windsurfing, boating, waterskiing, and sailing are all pursued at Cherry Creek. Specific areas for different sports are designated to avoid conflicts, and boats are limited to no more than 300 at a time.

Eight miles of paved bicycle and foot trails circle the reservoir, and another ten miles of foot and horse trails follow the creek. The park runs interpretive walks and talks by reservation. Picnic sites and the campground are open year-round, weather permitting. The park has a shooting range, model airplane field, dog training area, and handicapped fishing areas.

"We really work at maintaining the park's naturalness," says Dunlap. "People are always amazed to see mule deer, coyotes, or pheasants here." Cherry Creek is also, Dunlap notes, "a fantastic area for birdwatching."

Chatfield State Recreation Area, fifteen miles southwest of Denver, includes 1,150-acre Chatfield Reservoir, formed by a dam on the South Platte River. After pioneers settled along the river in the 1800s, a number of floods swept through. But the worst came on June 16, 1965, when the swollen South Platte rose over its banks, killing thirteen people and

causing $300 million in damages. Two years later the U.S. Army Corps of Engineers began dam construction. The resulting lake, leased to the Colorado Division of Parks and Outdoor Recreation, opened as a park in 1976.

Today the 5,200-acre park hosts over a million visitors every year. As at Cherry Creek, fishing is the most popular year-round activity. Spring brings superb trout fishing, while summer yields bass, perch, crappie, and catfish. As the lake cools in autumn, trout move back into the shallows. Fly fishermen match wiles with trout in the South Platte River south of the lake.

Almost twenty-five miles of paved trails follow the lakeshore for bicyclists and walkers. A horse trail crosses grassy fields on the west side of the park before entering Waterton Canyon. At the canyon, just outside the park, is the start of the 450-mile-long Colorado Trail to Durango. Other trails follow the South Platte upstream and through the Plum Creek Nature Area on the park's southeastern corner. Here visitors can see whitetail and mule deer, coyotes, rabbits, foxes, beaver, and over 180 species of birds.

A twenty-seven-acre heron rookery is Chatfield's most unusual wildlife area. Up to fifty pairs of great blue herons nest in the tops of dead cottonwood trees on the southwestern side of the lake. An observation deck gives, with binoculars, excellent views of these graceful birds. The rookery is closed during the summer

► *Perfect end to a perfect day: sunset limns clouds over Cherry Creek. Over thirty activities attract Denver residents here.* BRUCE W. HILL

► *Dancing on the wind, windsurfers make waves at Chatfield State Recreation Area southwest of Denver. The park offers outdoor sports for over a million visitors every year.*
STEWART M. GREEN

BOULDER PARKS

Unlike many Colorado cities, Boulder hasn't looked at endless suburban expansion as inevitable. Boulderites have always known their city had a distinct identity from Denver that needed to be preserved. Boulder's scenic assets were recognized as early as 1910 when Frederick Law Olmsted Jr. (whose father designed Central Park) wrote, "In the great tract of unspoiled foot-hill scenery, Boulder has a priceless possession." It took almost sixty years, however, before Olmsted's Boulder park plan became reality. Proposed development on the city's mountain backdrop in 1964 awakened citizens to the need for new parks. Three years later Boulder became the nation's first city to tax itself for the acquisition of parkland. Today Boulder County boasts over 32,000 acres of public parks and open space, Colorado's largest urban park system.

Boulder Mountain Park, the city's first, was started in 1898 when eighty acres were purchased for Chautauqua Park. In 1899 Congress granted 180 acres to Boulder for parkland, including Flagstaff Mountain, and in 1907 gave an additional 1,600 acres.

Today, 5,500-acre Boulder Mountain Park forms the nucleus of a three-unit, 7,000-acre mountain park system run by the City of Boulder's Parks and Recreation Department. The system includes Boulder Reservoir and Sawhill Ponds, a 240-acre wildlife preserve on the eastern edge of Boulder. The sixteen Sawhill ponds were created over a twenty-five-year period when the area along

nesting season to protect the birds; slight disturbances, even passing boats, can cause the herons to abandon their nests.

A campground, picnic grounds, a model airplane runway, the Montgolfier Launch Site for balloons, and a swim beach are other amenities. Water sports include boating, waterskiing, sailing, and windsurfing.

Because Cherry Creek and Chatfield are so popular, the park administrations have taken steps to preserve a quality experience. When enough cars enter to fill the parking spaces, they close the gates. Cars can enter when others leave. "It works out pretty well," says Dunlap. "Most visitors stay for half a day, so we have a morning crowd and an afternoon crowd."

Boulder Creek was dredged for gravel. Groundwater filled up the gravel pits, creating ponds ideal for waterfowl.

Boulder Mountain Park forms a magnificent backdrop to the city. Flagstaff, Green, and Boulder mountains dominate the view. The Flatirons, tilted sandstone slabs, hang on the sides of Green Mountain. All are popular with rock climbers, particularly the east face of the Third Flatiron, which climber Yvon Chouinard calls the "finest beginner's climb in the country." Boulder Mountain sports other sandstone slabs and several spires including Devil's Thumb.

Visitation for the Boulder Mountain Park system numbers over 1.5 million per year, with 65 percent of park visitors from outside Boulder County. "We're really like a small national park," says Mountain Park Ranger Brian Peck. "And we're fighting with the same dilemma as the National Park System—how do we manage and preserve our resource base without its being overused?" Peck points out that Boulder is paying for a regional park system used by many residents of the Denver metro area.

Flagstaff Mountain, its summit accessible by road, has the most visitors with 721,000 annually. Many, says Peck, "come for the drive." Others come for picnicking, climbing, and hang-gliding. Two hundred weddings are performed here every year. In other areas hikers and horseback riders share thirty-seven miles of trails, while climbers ascend the cliffs. No mountain biking is permitted.

This park also provides important plant

► *A dragonfly, one of the world's oldest insect species, balances atop wavering grass at Sawhill Ponds, a wildlife preserve in Boulder. Sixteen ponds along Boulder Creek provide shelter and food to a wide variety of mammals and birds.* STEWART M. GREEN

and animal habitat. Paper birch stands in Long Canyon mark the species' farthest southern extent in North America. Big bluestem grass, common to eastern Kansas, grows in mountain meadows. Some 1,100 mule deer live in the park and on surrounding open space, averaging sixty-five per square mile, about double Colorado's average deer population. Other animals include seventy-five mammal species and large concentrations of raptors—hawks, owls, prairie falcons, and golden and bald eagles.

Bordering the Mountain Park units are 16,100 acres managed by Boulder's Open Space Department. Started in 1967, Boulder Open Space is different from other national greenbelt and open space programs. Open Space District Supervisor Chris Wilson explains, "Over half our

property is in agricultural production—dryland crops, irrigated crops, ranching, and horse operations." The land, leased to local farmers and ranchers, remains open to public use except for a few isolated parcels with endangered wildlife species, biological study sites, or landowner restrictions. People use open space for hiking, biking, and horseback riding on eighty-five miles of trails. Anglers fish for trout along streamside corridors edging Boulder, South Boulder, and Fourmile creeks.

Scattered among the open space lands are 269 acres of tallgrass prairie designated as the Colorado Tallgrass Prairie Natural Area. Similar to tallgrass prairies on the moister eastern Great Plains, this grassland may be a remnant from 10,000 years ago when Colorado

was cooler and wetter than the present.

Since 1975 a third agency, Boulder County Parks and Open Space Department (the other two are the city's Parks and Recreation Department and Open Space Department), has been managing public parklands. Boulder County cares for 6,890 acres scattered in sixty-seven different properties.

Walker Ranch Park, at 2,556 acres, is the largest county park. Eight miles west of Boulder, it adjoins Boulder Mountain Park on the east, Eldorado Canyon State Park on the south, and Roosevelt National Forest on the west. Homesteaded in 1882 by James Walker, the property was obtained by Boulder County in 1976 to preserve it from encroaching subdivisions. Because of the ranch's historic value (an 1860s log cabin was

► *At sunrise, a solitary mule deer buck, antlers in velvet, crosses a meadow below Green Mountain in Boulder Mountain Park.* W. PERRY CONWAY

used as a stage stop for miners journeying from Boulder to Central City), 2,028 acres of the park are listed on the National Register of Historic Places—the largest listing in Colorado. Walker Ranch offers panoramic views, hiking and picnicking among its grassy meadows, ponderosa pine forests, and rock outcrops.

Rabbit Mountain Park is a 1,132-acre county park located fifteen miles north of Boulder off Colorado Highway 66. Rabbit Mountain is dry, rocky, and dominated by shrubs and grasses. Deer range across the park's open expanse. The tracks of secretive mountain lions are common here. Other animals include raptors, prairie dogs, and rattlesnakes. Arapahoe Indians wintered here, and eighty-nine tepee rings have been identified on Rabbit Mountain. Visitors enjoy views of the Indian Peaks on the Continental Divide and over three miles of trails.

Other county parklands include Bald Mountain Scenic Area above Left Hand

Canyon, 773-acre Betasso Preserve, Walden Ponds Wildlife Habitat adjacent to Sawhill Ponds east of Boulder, and popular Boulder Falls, the most heavily used county park, with more than 200,000 visitors a year.

Most Boulder County parks are not developed, but in the future residents can expect more facilities and trails, as well as an educational nature center near Longmont and a living history program at Walker Ranch.

"People use and appreciate our county parks," says Rich Koopman, the Boulder County Park's environmental resource manager. "If you look at a map of Boulder County, you can see all our lands. We'll still have those in the future, and we'll have the choice of what to do with them. A lot of other cities in the Denver metro area aren't buying parklands—they won't have that choice." Boulder residents know that and are already planning their future with the largest and best urban park and open space system in Colorado. That's their legacy to future Boulder residents. As Chris Wilson says, "Colorado cities need to plan for the future. There will always be potholes to fix, but once the mountain backdrop is gone, it's gone forever."

► *The Maiden towers over Boulder and the plains below. Here, a climber rappels down the spire's overhanging west face to an airy perch. In potholes atop the Maiden, intrepid biologists have found freshwater shrimp.* ED WEBSTER

COLORADO SPRINGS AND EL PASO COUNTY PARKS

▶ *A lone hiker surveys Bear Creek Canyon Park's wild domain from the Palmer Trail. One of eight natural parks, this Colorado Springs city park extends across ridges cloaked in ponderosa pine and Douglas fir.* STEWART M. GREEN

Colorado Springs was fortunate to have a visionary as its founder. General William Jackson Palmer, Civil War hero and railroad magnate, recognized from the city's founding in 1871 that parks were essential to every citizen's well-being. Through donations of land and money, he gave the city the foundation for its park system, including Palmer, Bear Creek Canyon, and North Cheyenne Canyon parks. The city's most famous park, Garden of the Gods, was donated in 1907 by the heirs of owner Charles W. Perkins to be "free and forever open to the public."

With Austin Bluffs, Pulpit Rock, Ute Valley, and Sonderman parks, the city's regional park system now encompasses eight parks with a total of 4,906 acres. These natural units, along with community parks and sports, cultural, and handicapped programs, are managed by the Colorado Springs Park and Recreation Department.

Both visitors and residents appreciate and use the city parklands. Annual visitation at Garden of the Gods, the only park that keeps such records, approaches 1.7 million. A quartet of parks—the Garden, North Cheyenne Canyon, Bear Creek Canyon, and Palmer—accounts for most visitor use and 85 percent of the park acreage. The city parks department manages the areas for hiking, rock climbing, picnicking, sightseeing, horseback riding, and nature study.

The Garden of the Gods, an extraordinary display of sandstone hogbacks, is the jewel in the Colorado Springs park system. An updated plan being formulated·by a citizen's advisory group calls for more preservation of the rocks and ecosystems, removal of some roads, and a new visitor center.

North Cheyenne Canyon, another spectacular city park, is a deep cleft carved by North Cheyenne Creek through pink granite cliffs. An 1893 travel brochure extolled the canyon's features: "Beautiful, picturesque, grand, and in places awe-inspiring are these stupendous gorges, awakening deepest emotions in all beholders." The park has excellent hiking trails, including a one-mile climb to the panoramic summit of Mount Cutler.

The other parks—Austin Bluffs, Pulpit Rock, Ute Valley, and Sonderman—are managed as open-space buffers against development. Rugged Pulpit Rock looms over northern Colorado Springs. The city offers nature programs and hiking trails in ninety-acre Sonderman Park. "It's surprisingly good wildlife habitat, with deer, owls, and lots of birds, for being so close to downtown," says Regional Parks Supervisor Rick Severson.

The Colorado Springs' parks department plans to acquire land on the east side of town where future growth will occur. "The Jimmy Camp Creek area will make a great park that either El Paso County Parks or we will develop," says Severson.

► *Fed by mountain snowmelt, Helen Hunt Falls tumbles over a bench of granite in North Cheyenne Canyon Park.* STEWART M. GREEN

► *Junior entomologists, right, study the day's insect catch at El Paso County's Bear Creek Nature Center. Educational exhibits and programs orient visitors to the park's plant and animal life.* STEWART M. GREEN

► *A park naturalist, far right, answers a family's wildflower questions during Bear Creek's traditional Spring Hike. Every May hundreds of walkers come to the park to explore Colorado mammals, plants, insects, reptiles, and ecology.*
STEWART M. GREEN

The El Paso County Parks Department manages six parks spread across El Paso County as well as the Barr Trailhead in Manitou Springs. Bear Creek Regional Park, nestled against the mountains west of Colorado Springs, is the county's largest with 1,275 acres. Much of Bear Creek is developed for recreation, including a rodeo stadium, equestrian center, eight tennis courts, an archery range, and three playing fields. The Bear Creek Nature Center, on the upper 150 acres of the park, offers exhibits and programs to orient visitors to the ecology of the Pikes Peak region. Two trails start at the center: one follows a lush creek bottom past cottonwoods, the other climbs through oak copses to dry meadows dotted with yucca.

Black Forest Regional Park, 240 acres, lies ten miles north of Colorado Springs in the Black Forest. The upper section is a natural area with an easy hiking trail through ponderosa pine woodland. Gentle terrain and heavy snowfall make this a popular cross-country ski area. The lower section of the park on Shoup Road has a grassy field and picnic shelters.

Fox Run Regional Park, twenty miles north of Colorado Springs, also protects a section of the Black Forest. Most of the 390-acre park is undeveloped, although there are playing fields, picnic pavilions, and two small lakes. Two miles of trails follow forested ridges that offer views of Pikes Peak.

The other county parks, Homestead Ranch and Fountain Creek, are currently undeveloped. Homestead Ranch, eighteen miles northeast of Colorado Springs, has meadows, cliffs, and woodlands tucked into its 380 acres. The Fountain Creek park will protect at least sixty acres of cottonwoods and creekside vegetation ten miles south of Colorado Springs. Trails and interpretative displays are planned for it as well.

OTHER URBAN PARKLANDS

Other Colorado cities own extensive park systems. Lakewood, on Denver's western doorstep, has over 1,200 acres spread through thirty-two parks and open space areas. Bear Creek Lake Park, surrounding Bear Creek Reservoir, is used for hiking, fishing, and horseback riding. The Bear Creek Greenbelt offers walking and bicycling paths, birdwatching, and the historic Stone House, a former stagecoach stop.

Larimer County, encompassing Fort Collins, Loveland, and Berthoud, owns fourteen parks and recreation areas totaling 8,843 acres. The most popular is 3,900-acre Horsetooth Reservoir Park on Fort Collins' western edge. Visitors boat, waterski, and fish on the 1,900-acre lake and camp, picnic, and hike on the sharp ridges bordering the lake. West of the reservoir lies scenic 2,100-acre Horsetooth Mountain Park, a spectacular area bordered on the north by Lory State Park. Horsetooth Mountain, purchased in 1982 through a county-wide sales tax, boasts a twenty-mile trail system to the hikers, horses, and mountain bicyclists, backcountry campsites, and Horsetooth

Rock, a familiar landmark in Larimer County. Other areas include Horsetooth Sports Cycle Park for all-terrain vehicles and motorcycles.

Pueblo has seventy-three parks, including its Arkansas River Trail that connects Lake Pueblo State Recreation Area's trail system to the nature center along the river.

Canon City, in cooperation with Colorado's Division of Parks and Outdoor Recreation, is developing Griffin Park along the Arkansas River with campsites, raft put-in and take-out areas, and a riverside trail system.

Colorado's urban parklands protect places of interest, natural areas, and recreational facilities. They have something for everybody, for picnickers, hikers, swimmers, water-skiers, fishermen, birdwatchers, runners, and even wilderness lovers. They all find their own park, their own special place to play, relax, and meditate. And why not? These are parks for people. ∎

FOR NOW AND FOR THE FUTURE

Where does Colorado go now? Our population is increasing, but park acreage, particularly along the Front Range, is not keeping pace. "Colorado needs more parks," says Chris Wilson, Boulder's Open Space supervisor. "A lot of people assume empty land is open space and parkland, until a developer starts to build on it. We need to protect more of that empty land, before we run out of elbowroom."

Various proposals have surfaced over the last few years to increase Colorado's park system. A western slope group has called on Congress to create a Black Canyon National Park or National Scenic Area that would dramatically increase the size of today's Black Canyon National Monument. Hovenweep National Monument has submitted proposals for future expansion to protect more Anasazi sites in southwestern Colorado. Bill Haase, a former BLM archaeologist, proposes a 400-acre Anasazi National Monument that would include Escalante Ruin, Lowry Pueblo National Historic Landmark, and four other major sites near Cortez.

The Colorado Division of Parks and Outdoor Recreation is quietly acquiring more parklands for the second-youngest state park system in the United States. "We have a need for more recreation areas," says Monica Miller, Director of Public Affairs for the state park system. Mancos State Recreation Area opened in the summer of 1987. Harvey Gap Reservoir near Glenwood Springs became a state recreation area in November 1987. "It's an ideal lake for windsurfing," says Miller. New additions for 1988 include Sylvan Lake State Recreation Area, south of Eagle, and Spinney Mountain State Recreation Area, west of Eleven Mile State Recreation Area. Other possible recreation areas include North Sterling Reservoir in Logan County and McPhee Reservoir near Dolores, as well as a proposed Arkansas River State Recreation Area stretching from Leadville to Lake Pueblo. No state parks will be acquired in the immediate future, but Staunton Ranch State Park, a scenic 1,720-acre mountain park west of Denver closed to public use, will open sometime in the 1990s. The park will be used for hiking, camping, and picnicking. The division of state parks wants to meet the challenge of Colorado's future with long-range planning. They know we need more parks and recreation areas, they know our population will continue climbing into the twenty-first century, and they know there is no better time to plan for the future than now.

As we wander through Colorado's majestic parklands, we discover threads of geology, ecology, history, and recreation that form a rich and complex tapestry. Colorado's parks are special places that teach us about ourselves and nature, that give us some of the state's best scenery, that allow us to find rest and relaxation. These parks are Colorado's priceless heritage, for now and for the future. Let's take care of them. ∎

► *Llamas pack visitors up to Thunder Lake in Rocky Mountain's wild backcountry. It's easy to have a wilderness experience in the park. The National Park Service limits overnight use in the popular areas to seven per site to preserve the park's solitude.*
JAMES FRANK

COLORADO PARKLANDS DIRECTORY

FEDERAL PARKLANDS

Black Canyon of the Gunnison National Monument

P.O. Box 1648
Montrose, CO 81402
(303) 249-9661

South rim is 11 miles east of Montrose off U.S. 50, open all winter; north rim is 14 miles south of Crawford off Colorado 92, road is graded dirt and closed in winter. 102 campsites on south rim, open May through October. Primitive campground on north rim. Visitor center on south rim. Sightseeing, hiking, rock climbing, fishing, backpacking, scenic drive. 20,763 acres. Entrance fee on south rim.

Colorado National Monument

Fruita, CO 81521
(303) 858-3617

East entrance is 4 miles east of Grand Junction off Colorado 340. West entrance is 10 miles west of Grand Junction off I-70, take Fruita exit to Colorado 340. 81 campsites in Saddlehorn Campground, open year-round. Visitor center is 4 miles from west entrance. Scenic drive, sightseeing, hiking, rock climbing, picnicking, backpacking, nature study. 20,450 acres. Entrance fee.

Curecanti National Recreation Area

P.O. Box 1040
Gunnison, CO 81230
(303) 641-2337

6 miles west of Gunnison on U.S. 50. 335 campsites. Camping, picnicking, hiking, backpacking, rock climbing, fishing, boating, sailing, sailboarding, scuba diving, hunting, ice fishing, cross-country skiing, boat tours on Morrow Point Lake, naturalist activities, interpretive exhibits, 3 visitor centers, marina. 42,114 acres. Entrance and camping fees.

Dinosaur National Monument

P.O. Box 210
Dinosaur, CO 81610
(303) 374-2216

Headquarters, visitor center, and entrance to Harper's Corner is 2 miles east of Dinosaur on U.S. 40. Dinosaur quarry is 7 miles north of Jensen off U.S. 40 in Utah. 134 campsites in 6 campgrounds, open year-round. Scenic drives, four-wheel drives, sightseeing, Dinosaur Quarry, visitor center, hiking, backpacking, fishing, river rafting, kayaking, horseback riding, rock climbing, nature study, birdwatching, picnicking, historical sites. 211,141 acres, part in Utah. Entrance fee to quarry area.

Escalante Ruin

Bureau of Land Management
Dolores, CO
(303) 882-3414 or 882-4811

2 miles west of Dolores on Colorado 184. Museum, hiking, sightseeing, picnicking. 40 acres. Free.

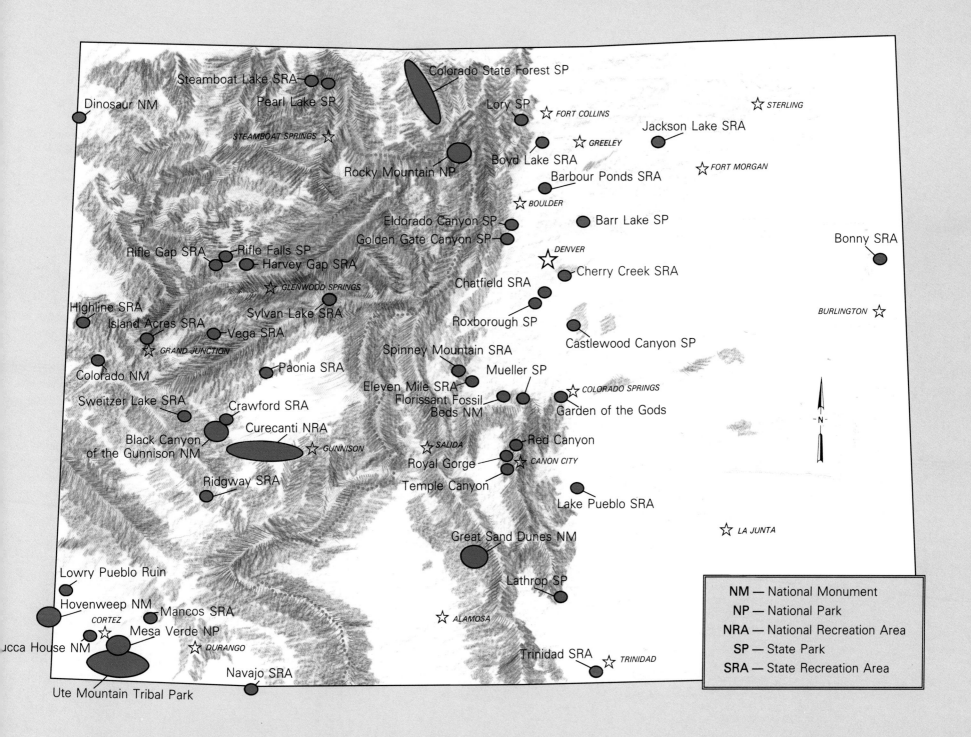

Steamboat Lake SRA
Pearl Lake SP
Dinosaur NM
Colorado State Forest SP
☆ STERLING
Lory SP
☆ FORT COLLINS
Jackson Lake SRA
STEAMBOAT SPRINGS ☆
☆ GREELEY
☆ FORT MORGAN
Boyd Lake SRA
Rocky Mountain NP
Barbour Ponds SRA
☆ BOULDER
Eldorado Canyon SP
Barr Lake SP
Golden Gate Canyon SP
Bonny SRA
Rifle Gap SRA
Rifle Falls SP
DENVER
Harvey Gap SRA
Cherry Creek SRA
Chatfield SRA
GLENWOOD SPRINGS ☆
Highline SRA
Sylvan Lake SRA
Roxborough SP
Island Acres SRA
Vega SRA
BURLINGTON ☆
GRAND JUNCTION ☆
Castlewood Canyon SP
Spinney Mountain SRA
Colorado NM
Paonia SRA
Mueller SP
Sweitzer Lake SRA
Eleven Mile SRA
☆ COLORADO SPRINGS
Crawford SRA
Florissant Fossil
Black Canyon
Curecanti NRA
Beds NM
Garden of the Gods
of the Gunnison NM
GUNNISON ☆
Red Canyon
☆ SALIDA
Ridgway SRA
Royal Gorge
☆ CANON CITY
Temple Canyon
Lake Pueblo SRA
-N-
☆ LA JUNTA
Great Sand Dunes NM
Lowry Pueblo Ruin
Lathrop SP
Hovenweep NM
Mancos SRA
CORTEZ
☆ ALAMOSA
Mesa Verde NP
ucca House NM
☆ DURANGO
Trinidad SRA
☆ TRINIDAD
Navajo SRA
Ute Mountain Tribal Park

NM — National Monument
NP — National Park
NRA — National Recreation Area
SP — State Park
SRA — State Recreation Area

Florissant Fossil Beds National Monument

P.O. Box 185
Florissant, CO 80816
(303) 748-3253

36 miles west of Colorado Springs, off U.S. 24 at Florissant. No camping. Visitor center, nature walks and talks, fossil display, hiking, cross-country skiing, wildlife study, horseback riding, picnicking. 5,992 acres. Entrance fee.

Great Sand Dunes National Monument

Mosca, CO 81146
(303) 378-2312

32 miles northeast of Alamosa. Reached via U.S. 160 and Colorado 150 from the south, or Colorado 17 and County Six Mile Lane from the west. Campground open April through October. Four-wheel drives, sightseeing, hiking, sand skiing, nature study, picnicking, visitor center. 38,400 acres. Entrance fee.

Hovenweep National Monument

c/o Mesa Verde National Park, CO 81330
(303) 529-4461

43 miles from Cortez via McElmo Canyon (Colorado 262), 45 miles from Cortez via U.S. 666 and Pleasant View. Approach roads are graded dirt. Visitor center at Square Tower Ruins. Campground (year-round). Hiking, sightseeing, picnicking. 785 acres, part in Utah. Free.

Lowry Pueblo Ruin

Bureau of Land Management
Dolores, CO
(303) 882-4811

20 miles northwest of Cortez off U.S. 160. Turn-off marked. Sightseeing, picnicking. 80 acres. Free.

Mesa Verde National Park

Mesa Verde National Park, CO 81330
(303) 529-4461 or 529-4465

8 miles east of Cortez off U.S. 160. Museum and visitor center. Guided tours in summer. Food, gas, and lodging from May through October. Morefield Campground: 477 campsites (May-October). Far View Lodge: 150 rooms. Hiking, sightseeing, picnicking, scenic drive. 52,000 acres. Entrance fee.

Rocky Mountain National Park

Estes Park, CO 80517
(303) 586-2371

65 miles northwest of Denver, via U.S. 34, U.S. 36, and Colorado 7. 750 campsites in 5 campgrounds, reservations in summer for Glacier Basin and Moraine Park. 3 visitor centers, nature walks and talks, picnicking, hiking, backpacking, rock climbing, ice climbing, mountaineering, cross-country skiing, fishing, wildlife study, horseback riding, scenic drives. 265,193 acres. Entrance fee.

Yucca House National Monument

c/o Mesa Verde National Park, CO 81330
(303) 529-4461

15 miles south of Cortez off U.S. 666. Officially closed, but instructions on visiting available at Mesa Verde. Sightseeing. No facilities. 10 acres. Free.

STATE PARKLANDS

Barbour Ponds State Recreation Area

3720 N. County Road 11-C
Loveland, CO 80537
(303) 669-1739

7 miles east of Longmont off Colorado 119 or 1 mile west of Interstate 25 at Exit 240. 60 campsites. Camping, picnicking, wakeless boating (20 horsepower or less), canoeing, fishing, hiking, nature study, hunting, interpretive programs. 143 acres. Entrance and camping fees.

Barr Lake State Park

13401 Picadilly Road
Brighton, CO 80601
(303) 659-6005

25 miles northeast of Denver on Interstate 76, Exit at Bromley Lane. No camping. Visitor center and nature center, hiking, picnicking, fishing, wakeless boating, wildlife study, birdwatching, nature walks and talks, horseback riding, cross-country skiing, waterfowl hunting. 2,610 acres. Entrance fee.

Bonny State Recreation Area

3010 County Road 3, Box 78-A
Idalia, CO 80735
(303) 354-7306

23 miles north of Burlington/I-70 off Colorado 385. 200 campsites. Camping, picnicking, fishing, boating, sailboarding, sailing, waterskiing, swimming, marina,

boat rental, nature study, hunting, cross-country skiing, ice fishing, interpretive programs. 6,900 acres. Entrance and camping fees.

Boyd Lake
State Recreation Area

3720 N. County Road 11-C
Loveland, CO 80537
(303) 669-1739

1 mile east of Loveland or 1 mile west of I-25 off Colorado 34. 148 campsites. Camping, picnicking, fishing, boating, sailing, waterskiing, swimming, sailboarding, marina, boat rental, hunting, cross-country skiing, ice fishing. 1,944 acres. Entrance and camping fees.

Castlewood Canyon State Park

13787 South Highway 85
Littleton, CO 80125
(303) 688-5242

30 miles south of Denver on Colorado 83. Park road is often closed in winter. No camping. Hiking, rock climbing, picnicking, birdwatching, cross-country skiing. 873 acres. Entrance fee.

Chatfield State Recreation Area

11500 N. Roxborough Park Road
Littleton, CO 80125
(303) 797-3986

15 miles southwest of Denver off Colorado 75. 153 campsites. Camping, picnicking, fishing, boating, sailing, sailboarding, swimming, waterskiing, marina, boat rental, hiking, horseback riding, horse rental, bicycling, model airplane field, nature study, birdwatching, ice fishing,

cross-country skiing, interpretive programs. 6,750 acres. Entrance and camping fees.

Cherry Creek
State Recreation Area

4201 S. Parker Road
Aurora, CO 80014
(303) 690-1166

1 mile south of I-225 off Parker Road. 102 campsites. Camping, picnicking, fishing, boating, sailing, sailboarding, waterskiing, swimming, marina, boat rental, hiking, horseback riding, horse rental, nature study, interpretive programs, bicycling, ice fishing, cross-country skiing, dog training area, model airplane field, birdwatching, 4,185 acres. Entrance and camping fees.

Colorado State
Forest State Park

Star Route Box 91
Walden, CO 80480
(303) 723-8366

75 miles west of Fort Collins on Colorado 14, over Cameron Pass. 113 campsites. Fishing, hiking, backpacking, boating, horseback riding, snowmobiling, cross-country skiing, hunting, ice fishing, cabin rental, mountain bicycling. 72,000 acres. Entrance and camping fees.

Crawford State
Recreation Area

P.O. Box 147
Crawford, CO 81415
(303) 921-5721

1 mile south of Crawford on Colorado

92. 55 campsites. Camping, picnicking, fishing, boating, waterskiing, swimming, sailboarding, hunting, ice fishing, interpretive programs. 1,289 acres. Entrance and camping fees.

Eldorado Canyon State Park

Box B
Eldorado Springs, CO 80025
(303) 494-3943

8 miles south of Boulder on Colorado 170. Rock climbing, hiking, sightseeing, picnicking, cross-country skiing. No camping. 848 acres. Entrance fee.

Eleven Mile State
Recreation Area

Star Route 2, Box 4229
Lake George, CO 80827
(303) 748-3401

49 miles west of Colorado Springs off U.S. 24. 274 campsites. Camping, picnicking, fishing, boating, windsurfing, hiking, hunting, snowmobiling, cross-country skiing, ice fishing, birdwatching, interpretive programs. No water contact sports allowed. 7,220 acres. Entrance and camping fees.

Golden Gate Canyon State Park

Route 6, Box 280
Golden, CO 80403
(303) 592-1502

30 miles west of Denver, via Golden Gate Canyon Road from Golden. 142 campsites. Hiking, backpacking, rock climbing, fishing, hunting, horseback riding, visitor center, scenic drive, picnicking. 8,787 acres. Entrance and camping fees.

Harvey Gap
State Recreation Area

c/o Rifle Gap SRA
0050 County Road 219
Rifle, CO 81650
(303) 625-1607

14.5 miles north of I-70 and Rifle interchange on County Road 237. Day-use only. Wakeless boating, fishing, excellent windsurfing, picnicking. 360 acres. Entrance fee.

Highline State Recreation Area

1800 11.8 Road
Loma, CO 81524
(303) 858-7208

8 miles north of I-70 and Loma, off Colorado 193. 25 campsites. Camping, picnicking, fishing, boating, waterskiing, sailboarding, swimming, canoeing, hiking, birdwatching, 918 acres. Entrance and camping fees.

Island Acres
State Recreation Area

P.O. Box B
Palisade, CO 81526
(303) 464-0548

5 miles east of Palisade, off I-70 (Exit 47). 32 campsites. Camping, picnicking, fishing, wakeless boating, canoeing, hiking, swimming, interpretive programs. 139 acres. Entrance and camping fees.

Jackson Lake
State Recreation Area

26363 County Road 3
Orchard, CO 80649
(303) 645-2551

10 miles north of I-76 and U.S. 34 interchange, off Colorado 39. 200 campsites. Camping, picnicking, fishing, boating, sailing, sailboarding, waterskiing, swimming, marina, boat rental, hunting, cross-country skiing, ice fishing, birdwatching, interpretive programs. 2,327 acres. Entrance and camping fees.

Lake Pueblo
State Recreation Area

640 Pueblo Reservoir Road
Pueblo, CO 81005
(303) 561-9320

6 miles west of Pueblo on Colorado 96. 223 campsites. Camping, picnicking, fishing, boating, sailing, waterskiing, sailboarding, swimming, marina, boat rental, hiking, horseback riding, model airplane field, nature study, birdwatching, visitor center, interpretive programs, hunting. 19,755 acres. Entrance and camping fees.

Lathrop State Park

70 County Road 502
Walsenburg, CO 81089
(303) 738-2376

3 miles west of Walsenburg on U.S. 160. 106 campsites. Camping, picnicking, boating, canoeing, waterskiing, swimming, sailboarding, hiking, hunting, ice fishing, nature study, visitor center, interpretive programs. 1,370 acres. Entrance and camping fees.

Lory State Park

708 Lodgepole Drive
Bellvue, CO 80512
(303) 493-1623

15 miles west of Fort Collins.

Backcountry camping only. Hiking, backpacking, horseback riding, rock climbing, picnicking, hunting, cross-country skiing, nature study, water sports on Horsetooth Reservoir. 2,419 acres. Entrance and camping fees.

Mancos State Recreation Area

c/o Navajo State Recreation Area
Box 1697
Arboles, CO 81121
(303) 883-2208

5 miles northeast of Mancos, off U.S. 160. 25 campsites. Camping, picnicking, fishing, boating, hiking, hunting, cross-country skiing, ice fishing. 550 acres. Entrance and camping fees.

Mueller State Park

P.O. Box 248
Divide, CO 80814
(303) 687-2366

25 miles west of Colorado Springs off Colorado 67 and Teller County 61. No camping at present. Day-use only. Hiking, cross-country skiing, wildlife study, rock climbing, fishing, horseback riding. 12,094 acres. Free.

Navajo State Recreaton Area

Box 1697
Arboles, CO 81121
(303) 883-2208

37 miles southwest of Pagosa Springs, off Colorado 151 at Arboles. 71 campsites. Camping, picnicking, fishing, boating, houseboating, sailing, waterskiing, sailboarding, marina, boat rental, hiking, horseback riding, airstrip, hunting, visitor center. 18,272 acres

(5,000 in Colorado). Entrance and camping fees.

Paonia State Recreation Area

c/o Crawford State Recreation Area
P.O. Box 147
Crawford, CO 81415
(303) 921-5721

15 miles east of Paonia on Colorado 133. 31 campsites. Camping, picnicking, fishing, boating, waterskiing, sailboarding, hunting, cross-country skiing, ice fishing. No drinking water. 1,816 acres. Entrance and camping fees.

Pearl Lake State Park

Box 750
Clark, CO 80428
(303) 879-3922

25 miles north of Steamboat Springs on County Road 129. 43 campsites. Camping, picnicking, fishing, wakeless boating, canoeing, hunting, snowmobiling, cross-country skiing, ice fishing. 274 acres. Entrance and camping fees.

Ridgway State Recreation Area

c/o Division of Parks & Outdoor Recreation
1313 Sherman Street, 618
Denver, CO 80203
(303) 866-3437

Currently closed. Scheduled to open in 1989 for camping, picnicking, boating, hiking, and other activities. 3,263 acres.

Rifle Falls State Park

0050 County Road 219
Rifle, CO 81650
(303) 625-1607

13 miles north of Rifle on Colorado 325. 18 campsites. Hiking, cross-country skiing, picnicking. 220 acres. Entrance and camping fees.

Rifle Gap State Recreation Area

0050 County Road 219
Rifle, CO 81650
(303) 625-1607

8 miles north of I-70 and Rifle interchange, on Colorado 325. 46 campsites. Camping, picnicking, fishing, boating, waterskiing, sailboarding, swimming, scuba diving, hunting, ice fishing. 2,421 acres. Entrance and camping fees.

Roxborough State Park

4751 N. Roxborough Drive
Littleton, CO 80125
(303) 973-3959

15 miles southwest of Denver. Reached via U.S. 85 and Titan Road. Hiking, nature study, visitor center, nature walks and talks, cross-country skiing, birdwatching, sightseeing. No camping. 1,598 acres. Entrance fee.

Spinney Mountain State Recreation Area

c/o Eleven Mile SRA
Star Route 2, Box 4229
Lake George, CO 80827
(303) 748-3401

7 miles west of Eleven Mile SRA on County Road 59. Day-use in summer only. Fishing, boating, picnicking. 5,520 acres. Entrance fee.

Steamboat Lake State Recreation Area

Box 750
Clark, CO 80428
(303) 879-3922

28 miles north of Steamboat Springs on County Road 129. 200 campsites. Camping, picnicking, fishing, boating, sailing, waterskiing, sailboarding, marina, boat rental, hiking, hunting, snowmobiling, cross-country skiing, ice fishing, interpretive programs. 2,557 acres. Entrance and camping fees.

Sweitzer Lake State Recreation Area

1735 E Road
Delta, CO 81416
(303) 874-4258

3 miles south of Delta off U.S. 50. No camping. Picnicking, fishing, boating, waterskiing, swimming, hunting, ice fishing. 210 acres. Entrance fee.

Sylvan Lake State Recreation Area

c/o Rifle Gap SRA
0050 County Road 219
Rifle, CO 81650
(303) 625-1607

15 miles south of I-70 at the Eagle Exit, on West Brush Creek Road. 47 campsites. Camping, picnicking, fishing, boating, ice-fishing, cross-country skiing, snowmobiling. 155 acres. Entrance and camping fees.

Trinidad State Recreation Area

RR 3 Box 360
Trinidad, CO 81082
(303) 846-6951

3 miles west of Trinidad on Colorado 12. 62 campsites. Camping, picnicking, fishing, boating, sailing, waterskiing, sailboarding, hiking, horseback riding, hunting, ice fishing, interpretive programs. 2,900 acres. Entrance and camping fees.

Vega State Recreation Area

Box 186
Collbran, CO 81624
(303) 487-3407

12 miles east of Collbran, off Colorado 330. 109 campsites. Camping, picnicking, hiking, fishing, boating, waterskiing, sailboarding, horseback riding, hunting, snowmobiling, cross-country skiing, ice fishing. 1,798 acres. Entrance and camping fees.

OTHER PARKLANDS

Boulder County Parks and Open Spaces

2045 13th Street
P.O. Box 471
Boulder, CO 80306
(303) 441-3950

67 different parklands, including Betasso Preserve, Bald Mountain Scenic Area, Walker Ranch Park, Rabbit Mountain Park, Walden Ponds Wildlife Habitat, Rock Creek Farm, and Boulder Falls. Hiking, camping, nature study, horseback riding, fishing, birdwatching, boating, bicycling, picnicking, interpretive programs. Maps and brochures available.

Boulder Mountain Parks

P.O. Box 791
Boulder, CO 80306
(303) 441-3408 or 441-3400

3 parks—Boulder Mountain Park, Sawhill Ponds, and Boulder Reservoir. Hiking, picnicking, jogging, rock climbing, fishing, boating, waterskiing, sailboarding, birdwatching, scenic views, nature study, interpretive programs, visitor center. Other Boulder Parks and Recreation parks include city parks, recreation centers, sports fields, and a golf course. Maps and brochures available.

Boulder Open Space Department

P.O. Box 791
Boulder, CO 80306
(303) 441-3440
Manages 16,100 acres surrounding Boulder, including Colorado Tallgrass Prairie Natural Area and White Rocks Natural Area. Hiking, bicycling, nature study, fishing, birdwatching, picnicking, jogging, horseback riding, rock climbing. Maps available.

Canon City Parks & Forestry Department

221 Griffin Avenue
Canon City, CO
(303) 275-5952

Royal Gorge: Bridge area developed for tourism—incline railway, aerial tramway, suspension bridge, sightseeing, hiking, picnicking. Rest of canyon is primitive—free camping, picnicking, hiking, rock climbing, river rafting, kayaking, nature study. 5,120 acres. Entrance fee to bridge. Red Canyon Park: Sightseeing, hiking, free camping, picnicking, nature study. 600 acres. Free. Temple Canyon Park: Sightseeing, hiking, fishing, free camping, picnicking, nature study, wading. 640 acres. Free.

Colorado Springs Park & Recreation Department

1401 Recreation Way
Colorado Springs, CO 80903
(303) 578-6640

Garden of the Gods, North Cheyenne Canyon, Palmer, Bear Creek Canyon parks. City parks, recreation centers, golf courses, sports fields, White House Ranch Historic Site, City Auditorium, Ski Broadmoor, Pioneer's Museum. Boating, fishing, hiking, nature study, horseback riding, bicycling, jogging, scenic views, skiing, cross-country skiing, rock climbing, interpretive programs, 2 visitor centers. Maps and brochures available.

Denver Parks & Recreation Department

1805 Bryant Street
Denver, CO 80204
(303) 575-2552

City parks, recreation centers, golf courses, recreational trail corridors, mountain parks, art museum, children's museum, botanic gardens, zoological gardens, Four Mile Historic Park, Mile

High Stadium, McNichols Arena, Winter Park Ski Area, Red Rocks Amphitheater. Sports fields, boating, rafting, fishing, hiking, nature study, bicycling, jogging, scenic views, horseback riding, cross-country skiing, downhill skiing.

El Paso County Parks Department

Bear Creek Nature Center
245 Bear Creek Road
Colorado Springs, CO 80906
(303) 520-6387

Bear Creek, Fountain Creek, Homestead Ranch, Black Forest, and Fox Run regional parks. Palmer Lake Regional Recreation Area. Barr Trailhead. Sports fields, boating, fishing, hiking, nature study, interpretive programs, horseback riding, bicycling, cross-country skiing. Maps and brochures available.

Jefferson County Open Space

18301 W. 10th Avenue, #100
Golden, CO 80401
(303) 278-5925

28 county parklands, including Hiwan Homestead Museum, Hogback, Mt. Falcon, White Ranch, Reynolds, Van Bibber, South Table Mountain, and Mt. Glennon parks. Hiking, backpacking, fishing, picnicking, horseback riding, nature study, scenic views, bicycling, cross-country skiing, boating, sports fields, interpretive programs. Maps and brochures available.

Larimer County Parks Department

1800 S. County Road 31

Loveland, CO 80537
(303) 669-4077

14 county parklands, including Horsetooth Mountain Park, Horsetooth Reservoir, Carter Lake, Pinewood Lake, Big Thompson parks. Picnicking, hiking, camping, backpacking, mountain bicycling, swimming, fishing, boating, sailboarding, sailing, scuba diving, marina, historic sites, ORV track, rifle range. Daily permit required at some parks. Maps available.

Ute Mountain Tribal Park

Towaoc, CO 81334
(303) 565-3751 Ext. 282

Tours start at Ute Mountain Pottery 15 miles south of Cortez on U.S. 666. Tours by reservation only. Tour is 100 miles round-trip. Hiking, backpacking, camping, sightseeing, mountain biking, tours to remote sites, horsepacking. 125,000 acres. Fees depend on length of tour and activity. Tips advised for guides.

Also available in the Colorado Geographic Series

*The Rivers of Colorado,
Book One*

by Jeff Rennicke

Here is the story of Colorado's 100 magnificent rivers told with 111 full-color photographs, maps, diagrams, charts, and a text filled with fascinating facts and amusing historical anecdotes. Gold-medal trout streams, the serene beauty of slick-water rivers, roaring white water—the world of Colorado's rivers will inform and fascinate you.

112 pages, 11'' x 8 1/2'', $14.95 softcover, $24.95 hardcover.

*Colorado Mountain Ranges,
Book Two*

by Jeff Rennicke

Dazzling color photographs of mountain peaks, wildlife, and wildflowers are the hallmark of this beautiful book. The geology that made Colorado's mountains possible, the natural history that brings them to life, and the recreation that makes them so much fun are presented in 135 beautiful color photos and an informative text.

128 pages, 11'' x 8 1/2'', $14.95 softcover, $24.95 hardcover.

*Pikes Peak Country,
Book Three*

by Jim Scott

From cosmopolitan Colorado Springs to the amazing Florissant fossil beds, Book Three explores the unique area around Pikes Peak in a lively, informative text and 150 color photos. For history buffs, outdoor enthusiasts, residents, and visitors, Colorado's most prominent peak and its surroundings are presented as never before in *Pikes Peak Country*.

104 pages, 11'' x 8 1/2'', $14.95 softcover, $24.95 hardcover.

*Colorado Ski Country,
Book Four*

by Charlie Meyers

Lavish color photos by the finest ski photographers and text by the *Denver Post*'s Charlie Meyers bring Colorado's ski country to your living room. "This book is full of great words and great skiing stories, and it is all done in a style that Charlie does better than anyone—with humor and affection and, above all, class."—William Oscar Johnson, Senior Editor, *Sports Illustrated*

104 pages, 11'' x 8 1/2'', $14.95 softcover, $24.95 hardcover.

Coming soon

Colorado Wildlife, Book Six

Falcon Press presents the most complete roundup ever of the animals of Colorado. With delightful photos by America's best wildlife photographers and an easy-to-read text filled with interesting and little known facts, *Colorado Wildlife* is sure to please the whole family.

To order

The Rivers of Colorado, Colorado Mountain Ranges, Pikes Peak Country, Colorado Ski Country, Colorado Parklands

Call toll-free—1-800-582-BOOK—to order with Visa or Mastercard. Or send a check or money order and include $1.50 postage and handling for each book to Falcon Press, P.O. Box 1718, Helena, MT 59624.

OUR GUARANTEE: *If you are not satisfied with any book obtained from Falcon Press, simply return your purchase for a full refund.*